A Guide to Historic *Winter Park*

A Guide to Historic Winter Park

Florida

Steve Rajtar & Gayle Prince Rajtar

The History Press

Published by The History Press
Charleston, SC 29403
www.historypress.net

Cover image: Knowles Memorial Chapel on the campus of Rollins College.
Photo by Gayle Prince Rajtar.

First published 2008

Manufactured in the United States

ISBN 978.1.59629.436.3

Library of Congress Cataloging-in-Publication Data

Rajtar, Steve, 1951-
A guide to historic Winter Park / by Steve Rajtar and Gayle Prince Rajtar.
p. cm.
Includes bibliographical references and index.
ISBN 978-1-59629-436-3
1. Winter Park (Fla.)--Tours. 2. Historic buildings--Florida--Winter Park--Guidebooks. 3. Historic sites--Florida--Winter Park--Guidebooks. 4. Architecture--Florida--Winter Park--Guidebooks. 5. Neighborhood--Florida--Winter Park--Guidebooks. 6. Walking--Florida--Winter Park--Guidebooks. 7. Winter Park (Fla.)--Buildings, structures, etc.--Guidebooks. 8. Winter Park (Fla.)--Pictorial works. 9. Winter Park (Fla.)--History. I. Rajtar, Gayle Prince. II. Title.
F319.W79R35 2008
917.59'23--dc22
2008011290

Contents

Introduction

When drivers cross the city limits to enter Winter Park, they are met by signs that say "Please drive with extraordinary care." The signs provide a hint as to what Winter Park was intended to be by its founders, and which it remains. Winter Park is "extraordinary."

The early 1880s were a time when well-to-do industrialists had just discovered Florida as an ideal place to spend their winters. A warm climate, opportunities for hunting and fishing and clean water for swimming and boating offered a break from the snow and bleak skies of New England and the Midwest.

Loring Chase and Oliver Chapman laid out a town among lakes and canals, and Northerners purchased large tracts and built magnificent homes. Some retained their ties to factories and offices north of the Mason-Dixon line, but many (especially those who suffered from chronic illnesses and sought a milder climate) became full-time residents of Winter Park.

Not long after the town was founded, it acquired a college worthy of the class of people who lived near it. It attracted the support of the local citizenry because it was more like an Ivy League school than a Southern state university. It taught classical languages and literature rather than agriculture and mining. The establishment of Rollins College attracted even more leaders of industry to the area. In other words, it attracted money.

One must drive with extraordinary care, not only because the narrow streets are not designed for speeding through the city, but also because there is so much to see. The homes and churches and other sights are worth the careful drive or the walk through neighborhoods that continue to maintain their extraordinary appearances.

The following pages will guide you through the years from the area's first settlers through its growth into a city that strives to retain its small-town appearance with an extraordinary character. It will also lead you from site to site within five sections of Winter Park, including the college campus, to trace the history of what remains and hopefully of what will still be there decades from now.

Part I

Highlights of Winter Park History

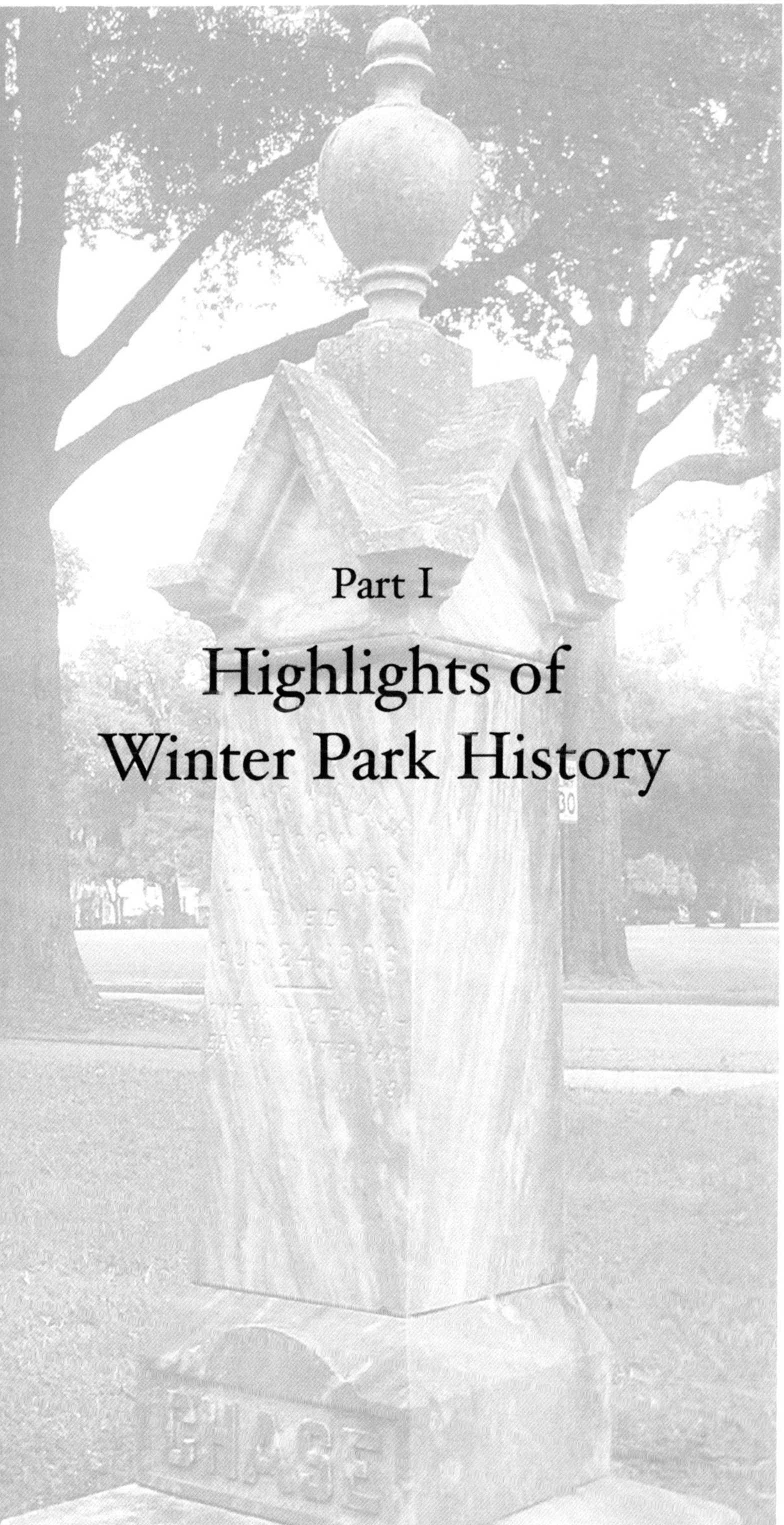

The 1850s

David Mizell

David W. Mizell arrived from Alachua County in 1858 with horses, cattle, hogs, turkeys and goats and bought eight acres from Isaac Rutland. Mizell built a log cabin on the eastern shore of Lake Osceola and named his settlement Lake View. He grew cotton and became the first chairman of the county board of commissioners.

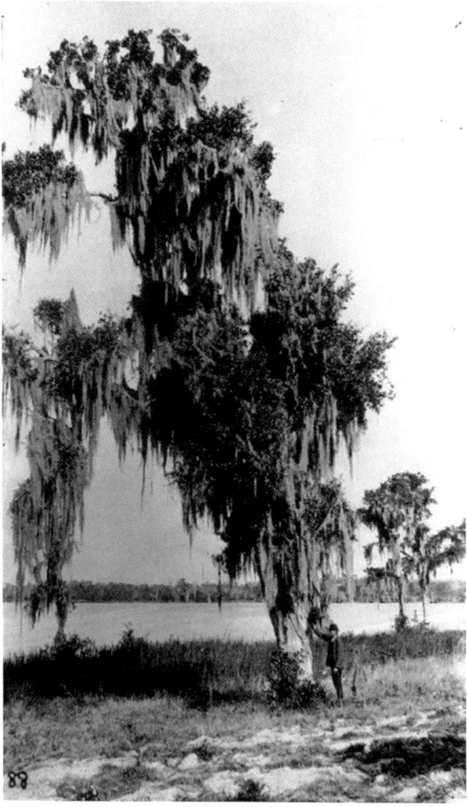

LAKE VIRGINIA
When early settlers arrived, they found lakes surrounded by tall trees and full of wildlife. A plant foreign to many newcomers was Spanish moss, an epiphyte (a plant that lives on other plants) that is usually found hanging in long, beardlike clumps, as in this photo from the 1880s. *Courtesy of the Florida Photographic Collection.*

The 1860s

James Harper

James E. and Mary Harper Jr. were residents of Atlanta. During the Civil War, he served in a Georgia regiment, but after the war ended, they settled in the portion of Winter Park now known as Orwin Manor, homesteading forty acres. The Harpers owned and operated a dairy farm and an orange grove.

The 1870s

Osceola

In 1870, Lake View was renamed Osceola for a Seminole chief who some believe once camped nearby. A post office was set up in the home of Colonel E.B. Livingston, who also kept a stock of groceries for sale. Osceola became a part of the town of Winter Park when it incorporated in 1887.

William Comstock

One of the early visitors to Osceola was William C. Comstock, who arrived in 1876 from Chicago, where he was in the grain business and served as the president of the Chicago Board of Trade. He built Eastbank, his winter home, along Lake Osceola in 1883. He served as a director of the Winter Park Company and a trustee of Rollins College and was an organizer of the Winter Park Library.

The 1880s

Railroad Tracks

Winter Park became connected to Sanford and points north by the tracks of the South Florida Railroad, which reached the area in July 1880. The railroad had been founded that year by the R.M. Pulsifer & Co., led by Royal M. Pulsifer, an owner of the *Boston Herald*. Across Old England Avenue from the country club is a small park containing the Pulsifer Place monument honoring him and the assistance he provided to the founders of Winter Park.

CHASE AND CHAPMAN

In 1881, Loring A. Chase of Chicago visited the area and convinced his boyhood friend, Oliver E. Chapman of Massachusetts, of the area's potential. Chase and Chapman bought six hundred acres from Colling R. Swope, Hiram Potter and Lawson Chase for a total of $13,000.

The two men had the area surveyed and named it Winter Park on August 29, 1881, intending it as a winter retreat for Northerners. Streets were laid out with ample space for parks, schools, hotels, a business district and a separate area for black residents. They advertised their new town throughout the eastern United States.

Before the end of 1881, a road connected with Osceola. At the time, Winter Park's population consisted of twelve families. Within three years, it grew to six hundred people. By 1885, there were several businesses and sixty-three dwellings, including the winter home of Alonzo W. Rollins, whose donation of cash and real estate was instrumental in the selection of Winter Park as the site for Rollins College. That same year, the Chase and Chapman partnership was dissolved when Chase bought out Chapman's share for $40,000.

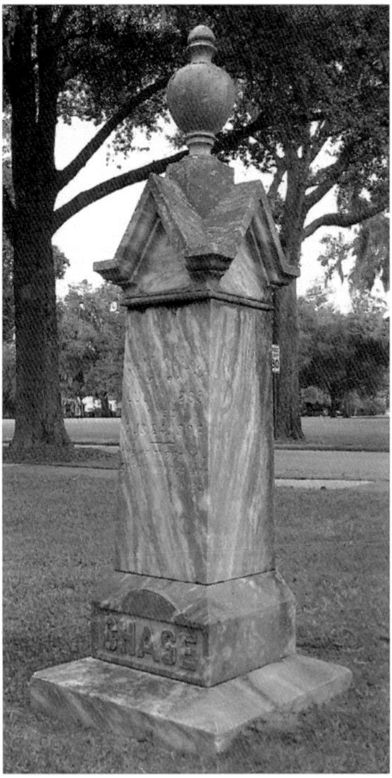

LORING CHASE
Loring Chase suffered from catarrh (inflammation of the nose and throat) and bronchitis, so he moved to Florida hoping that the climate would improve his health. It did, and he also saw an opportunity to create a town that would attract men and women of intelligence, culture, character, taste and means. *Photo by Steve Rajtar.*

RAILROAD STATION

When Loring Chase visited the area in 1881, there was a crude freight platform where the railroad tracks crossed New England Avenue, a convenient loading site for lumber dressed at the sawmill of John K. Coiner on the north shore of Lake Virginia. In 1882, a new passenger depot was dedicated at the Morse Boulevard crossing. It was the first commercial building completed in town. Inside, a telegraph office opened on January 1, 1883, with J.H. Willies serving as its operator and depot master.

In 1913, a new depot opened to serve the Atlantic Coast Line on the west side of the tracks. The Board of Trade billed its opening as "Town Improvement Day."

ROGERS HOUSE

The first hotel, the Rogers House, opened at 100–106 South Interlachen Avenue with twenty guest rooms on April 8, 1882. At the time, Winter Park had no real roads, just sandy trails through the woods. A second-floor rear room housed J.F. Welbourne's law office.

In 1904, Charles H. Morse purchased the hotel and donated it to Rollins College. A veranda was added, overlooking Lake Osceola, and it was renamed the Seminole Inn. It became

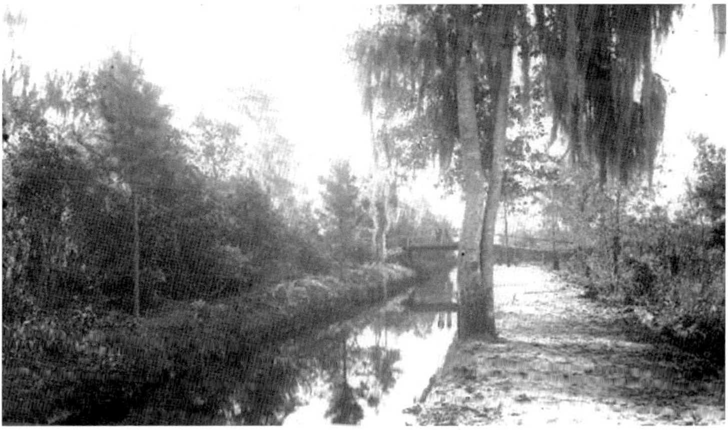

CANALS

Initially, canals dug to connect the lakes were straight so that logs could be floated to sawmills. This southward view from the 1880s is of the canal connecting Lakes Osceola and Virginia. The canals have been made more interesting by allowing them to wind through dense foliage, with exquisite homes and beautiful parks located along their routes. *Courtesy of the Florida Photographic Collection.*

The Inn in 1912 and the college sold it to Reuben P. Foley. In 1915, it was renamed the Virginia Inn, a name that it kept until it was torn down in 1966. In its place was built the Cloisters Condominiums.

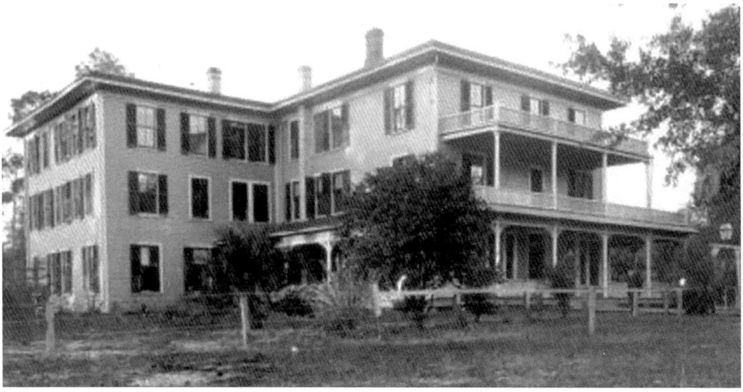

ROGERS HOUSE

Winter Park's first hotel began with twenty rooms for guests, and the first night's contingent included Loring Chase and Oliver Chapman and his family. By the time this photo was taken in the 1890s, the hotel had doubled in size and rooms were let for $10.00 to $17.50 per week. *Courtesy of the Florida Photographic Collection.*

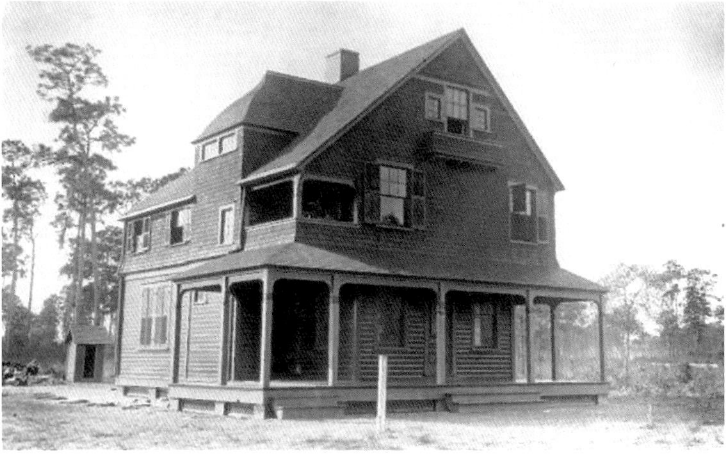

WINTER PARK COMPANY

Frederick Lyman and other astute businessmen formed the Winter Park Company to plan the town and its attractions, such as the Seminole Hotel. Pictured here from the mid-1880s was the company's office building, one of the earliest structures erected in downtown Winter Park. *Courtesy of the Florida Photographic Collection.*

FREDERICK LYMAN

In 1882, Frederick W. Lyman made his first visit to Winter Park. He was a founder of the First Congregational Church and is one of the pair credited with suggesting the establishment of a college. He was a director and the president of the Winter Park Company and was involved in the establishment of the Seminole Hotel. He served as a Rollins trustee and donated the school's first gymnasium in 1890.

FIRST CONGREGATIONAL CHURCH OF WINTER PARK

The first Congregational service in Winter Park was held by Reverend S.B. Andrews in the town hall on October 8, 1882. The Winter Park Congregational Church organized in 1884, and charter members included Methodists, Episcopalians, Congregationalists and Unitarians.

The first sanctuary was built in 1885, facing New England Avenue. The Hooker Memorial House opened in 1907 and served in a variety of ways, including housing the Duprey Memorial Kindergarten, which was started in 1916, and the Webster Kindergarten, started in 1927. The building was moved to Hannibal Square in 1940. Also in 1940, in its place, the present Hooker Hall was built to hold the Sunday school and parish activities.

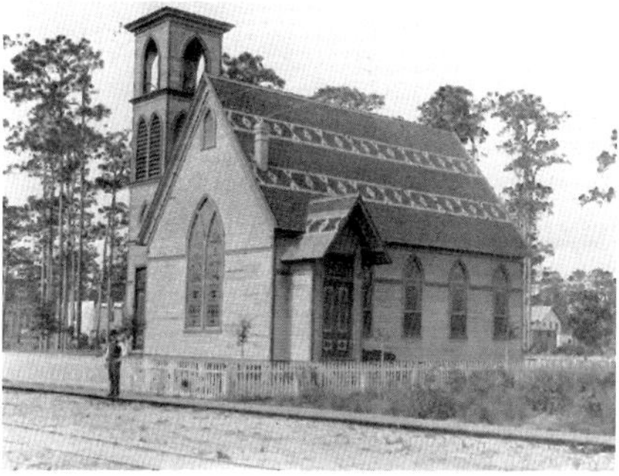

FIRST CONGREGATIONAL CHURCH

Shown here is the Congregational Church shortly after it was built in 1884. It was the first church erected in Winter Park and the minister who supervised its organization, Dr. Edward P. Hooker, served as the first president of Rollins College. *Courtesy of the Florida Photographic Collection.*

PRESIDENTIAL VISIT

On April 10, 1883, President Chester A. Arthur, who had been invited by Judge Lewis H. Lawrence, visited Winter Park. The new town's reputation was given a boost by some of Arthur's comments, including: "This is the prettiest spot I have seen in Florida, and I would like to rest under one of these grand old pines for a week."

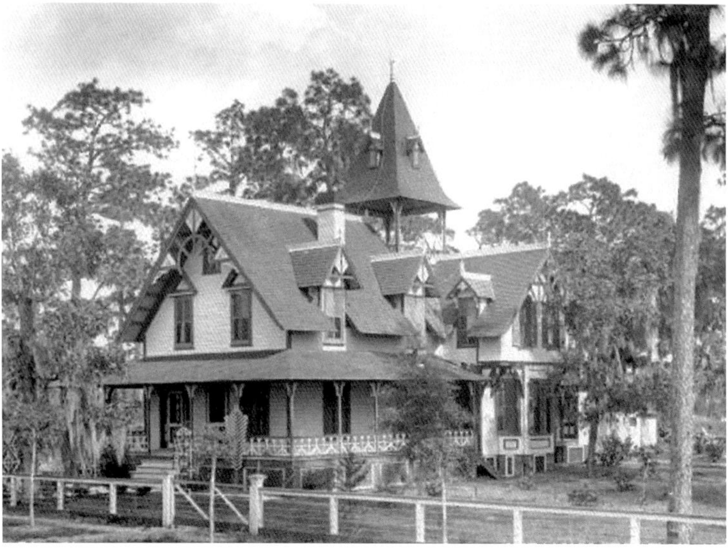

Welbourne House
Three years before this 1886 photo was taken, Judge J.F. Welbourne had this Victorian-style home built on the east side of Interlachen Avenue. Towering above it was an open belfry with a pyramidal cap. After 1884, it was acquired by William Waddell, who lived in it until 1910, when he moved it across the street and converted it into the Osceola House boardinghouse. It became part of the Congregational Church grounds in 1968. *Courtesy of the Florida Photographic Collection.*

Francis Knowles

Francis B. Knowles of Massachusetts first visited Florida in 1883 and met with an old friend, scale manufacturer Colonel Franklin Fairbanks, who told him about Winter Park. In 1885, Knowles returned and became a director and the largest stockholder of the Winter Park Company, which was formed to develop the town. He also served as a member of the first board of trustees of Rollins College, which named its first building Knowles Hall in his honor in 1886. Knowles also became the largest stockholder of the Seminole Hotel and controlled the Dinky Line railroad.

First United Methodist Church of Winter Park

This church was organized in 1885. Early services were held in the Congregational Church and members' homes, and then in Alexander Earl's building on Park Avenue. Reverend Henry J. Walker was chosen as its first pastor. Later, the congregation rented White's Hall.

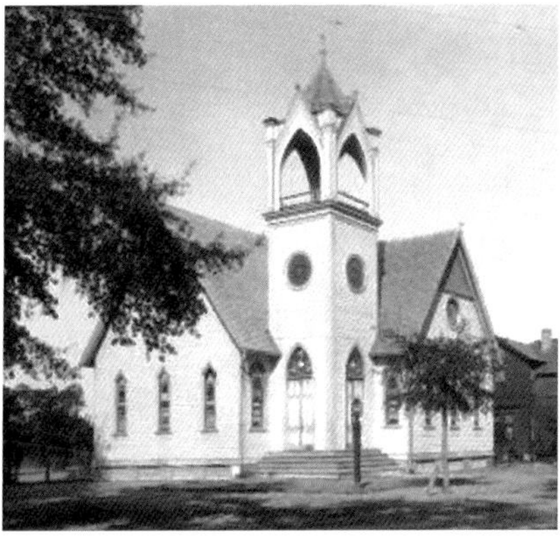

METHODIST EPISCOPAL CHURCH
In 1893, William Kirkpatrick donated a lot for construction of the Methodist church, whose cornerstone was laid on April 12, 1895. The entire church, designed by pastor Reverend John H. Martin, cost $3,000 to build and was dedicated on April 5, 1896. This photo was taken later that decade. *Courtesy of the Florida Photographic Collection.*

In 1922, the original sanctuary was moved to the west and turned ninety degrees to face Morse Boulevard. A new sanctuary was built in its place. The old parsonage was moved to the north to create a *U*-shaped group of buildings. The Wesleyan Building fronting on Morse Boulevard was completed in 1949 to house the Sunday school, and a two-story, *U*-shaped education building named Asbury Hall was erected in 1956.

SEMINOLE HOTEL

The Seminole Hotel attracted wealthy visitors and was served by two steam yachts, the *Alice*, which launched on Lake Osceola,

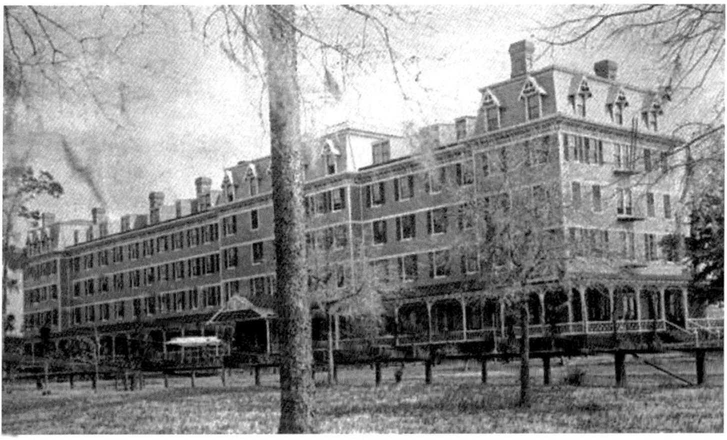

SEMINOLE HOTEL
One of the first acts of the Winter Park Company was to contract with Francis Knowles to build the Seminole Hotel between Lakes Osceola and Virginia. Knowles loaned $150,000 for the project, and the first brick was laid on March 26, 1885. This photo was taken about a decade following its 1886 grand opening. *Courtesy of the Florida Photographic Collection.*

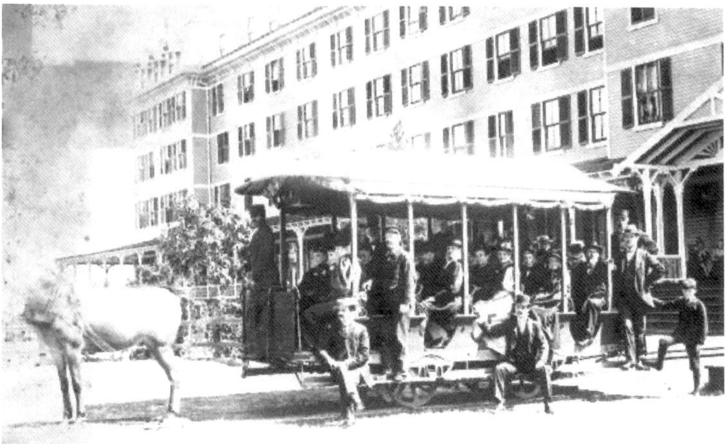

HORSE-DRAWN TROLLEY
The Seminole Hotel was served by a mule-drawn trolley called the Seminole Hotel Horse Car, enabling guests who arrived at the train station to merely switch to a second rail transport headed directly to the resort. *Courtesy of the Florida Photographic Collection.*

and the *Fanny Knowles*, which launched on Lake Virginia. Tracks for a mule-drawn trolley were laid in the roadbed of New England Avenue, connecting the railroad depot to the hotel in 1885. The tracks were later extended to the Dinky Depot on Ollie Avenue. The five-story Seminole Hotel with its 250 rooms was the largest hotel in Florida when it opened on January 1, 1886. It was heated with steam and accommodated up to four hundred guests.

ALL SAINTS EPISCOPAL CHURCH

The church was founded in 1886 and its original building was completed in 1891. The Ella K. Comstock Memorial Rectory and the Harriett Street Switzer Memorial Parish House were added in 1925.

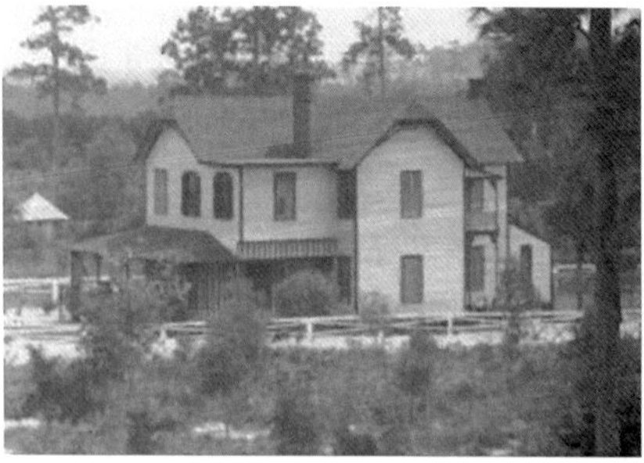

WHIPPLE HOUSE
One prominent local Episcopalian was Bishop Henry B. Whipple. Shown here is his large home, which he occupied by the mid-1880s. Previously, while serving in Minnesota, he convinced President Lincoln to pardon 265 Dakota Sioux who had been involved in the 1862 Dakota Conflict. *Courtesy of the Florida Photographic Collection.*

The new sanctuary building at 338 East Lyman Avenue held its first service in 1942. Architect Harold Hair of Winter Park used a Gothic design. The bell tower, offices and a two-story education building with twenty-four classrooms seating four hundred were built in 1964.

HANNIBAL SQUARE

The initial plat provided for a segregated black section, which became the community of Hannibal Square. It was included in the 1887 incorporation of Winter Park, but was officially detached after a stormy debate in 1893.

Hannibal Square developed its own churches and schools. The first church was built in 1884 with the help of the white Congregational Church. Surrounding lots were made available to "Negro families of good character who can be depended upon to work in the family or in the groves." Methodist and Baptist Missionary churches were built the following year. In 1891, the Chase-Moore Literary Club was organized in Hannibal Square and was presided over by Gus C. Henderson.

INCORPORATION

The Town of Winter Park incorporated in 1887 with Robert White Jr. as its first mayor. Osceola was included, as was Hannibal Square. At the time, 51 families were from the South and 141 were from the North, broken down as 57 Democrats and 133 Republicans. That same year, the first Winter Park newspaper was established, called the *Lochmede*. Winter Park became an incorporated city in 1925.

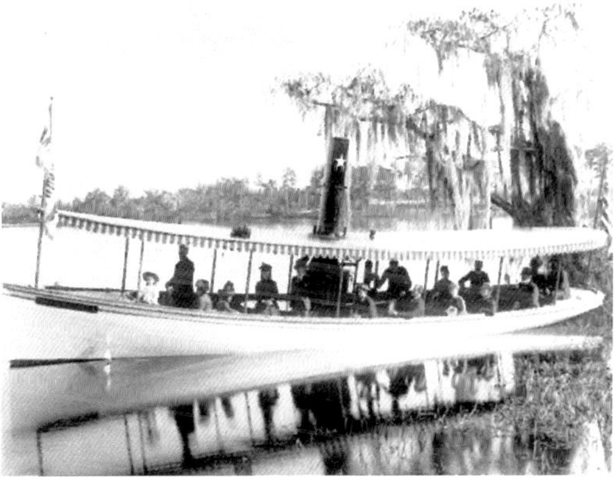

STEAM LAUNCH
Pictured here from the late 1880s was the *Fanny Knowles*, named for Frances Knowles Warren, the daughter of Francis Knowles. This boat launched from the south side of the hotel onto Lake Virginia, the most convenient water route to the college and the Dinky Line railroad station. *Courtesy of the Florida Photographic Collection.*

TOWN IMPROVEMENT ASSOCIATION

In 1887, the Town Improvement Association organized with goals of planting trees, repairing sidewalks, keeping parks maintained and encouraging residents to be sociable. In 1893, the name was changed to the Winter Park Village Improvement Association.

BROWN AND MCCLURE

Mary E. Brown and Mary McClure, teachers at Northwestern University, arrived in about 1880. At their home, which they called No Man's Land, they opened a school for black children and adults called New Hope Cottage. Classes began on January 1, 1888, and continued into the following year, when a school for black children opened in Hannibal Square.

Brown and McClure also constructed a building in 1888 in which they started a Congregational Sunday school for black residents. The pair served on the governing boards of the city hospital and library. After McClure's death, Brown razed No Man's Land and built a home she called The Hermitage near the intersection of Comstock and Chase Avenues.

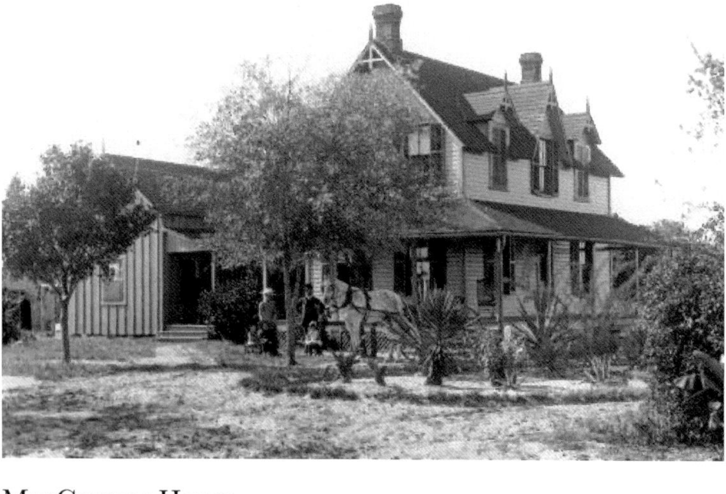

MACCOLLUM HOUSE

Although most early settlers came from New England and the Midwest, Winter Park also attracted people from areas farther away. Shown here in the mid-1880s is the home of Hugh MacCollum from Scotland, a lawyer who also became involved in the real estate profession. *Courtesy of the Florida Photographic Collection.*

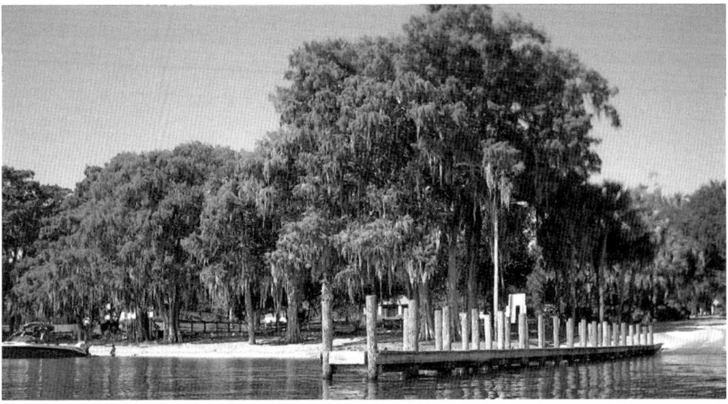

DINKY DOCK
Dinky Dock provides easy access for boaters to enter the chain of lakes and canals. The sand beach installed by the city in 1948 is a popular place to swim. The wooden depot stood at the left edge of this scene until it was torn down in 1967, and the tracks heading southwest through campus and north on their way to Oviedo were taken up in 1969. The Rotary Club purchased the site and donated it to the city to be used as a public park. *Photo by Steve Rajtar.*

THE DINKY LINE

The Winter Park Company granted J. Harry Abbott a railroad right of way in 1887. Its formal opening took place on January 2, 1889, with the arrival of a train from Orlando. The fare from that city was fifteen cents and the six-mile trip took a half hour.

The railroad soon was extended eastward through the college campus along the Lake Virginia shoreline and along Phelps and Ollie Avenues, and a depot was built in 1889 at the foot of Ollie Avenue. The railroad also ran eastward to Lake Charm in Oviedo beginning in 1891. In about 1900, the railroad was purchased by the Seaboard Air Line.

It was nicknamed the Dinky Line because of the creaking, screeching noises it made when rounding bends, plus its fragile qualities. Frequent stops were made for repairs and picking flowers. Its two pitch pine–burning engines were nicknamed "Tea Pot" and "Coffee Pot" and the train was often referred to as the "Little Wiggle."

GUS HENDERSON

Gus C. Henderson, who had moved to Hannibal Square in 1886, was a founder of the South Florida Colored Printing & Publishing Co. and was a strong advocate of incorporation. He encouraged fellow black residents to vote in favor of the formal establishment of Winter Park. Two years later, Henderson founded the *Advocate*, a newspaper edited by Reverend S.A. Williams for those living to the west of the railroad tracks. It gave black residents a forum for political discussion and continued publication until 1891.

The 1890s

KNOWLES PUBLIC SCHOOL

A wooden school opened at the southwest corner of Park and Canton Avenues for white children on February 11, 1890, on a site donated by Francis Knowles. By 1902, the student body had grown to fifty and was taught by two teachers. A new building replaced it in 1907, and remodeling in 1923 turned it into the Winter Park Hotel. For a time, it served as a men's college dormitory, and in 1949 it was reopened as a hotel, later being converted into a store.

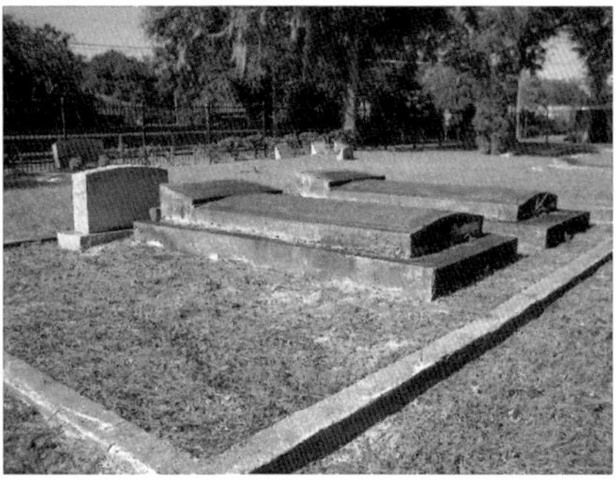

PINEYWOOD CEMETERY
The Pineywood (also known as Pinewood and Piney Woods) Cemetery for black residents was established in 1890 about three miles southeast of downtown. Its twelve acres were platted by railroad superintendent J. Harry Abbott. Plots originally sold for twenty-five cents each. *Photo by Steve Rajtar.*

WINTER PARK LIBRARY

The library was the outgrowth of a reading circle of nine women led by Elizabeth R. Hooker in 1885. The Winter Park Library Association located its small collection of books on the porch and hall belonging to Evaline Lamson at 503 Interlachen Avenue. It incorporated in 1893 and moved into a permanent home in 1902. That building was expanded several times, and in 1979 the library's collections were moved to a new building at 460 East New England Avenue. The old building was sold to the Episcopal Church.

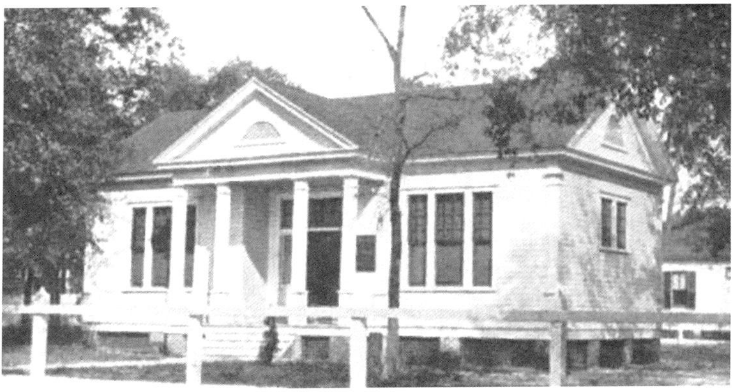

PUBLIC LIBRARY
After keeping its books in temporary quarters, the city's first library building was erected in 1902 along Interlachen Avenue on land donated by the Francis Knowles estate. This photo was taken about five years after the library moved into that building. *Courtesy of the Florida Photographic Collection.*

BIG FREEZE

In 1894, just after Christmas, Central Florida's citrus groves were damaged by a major freeze, just three days after a period of eighty-degree temperatures. After thirty-six hours, the cold subsided and some of the trees began to recover during a warm and wet January.

A second freeze hit on February 7, 1895, killing most of the trees. Temperatures dipped to the coldest reported up to that time. Sap froze inside the trunks, splitting many open with pops resembling gunshots, causing them to crash to the ground. Many growers left the area or turned to other businesses, and those who remained in the citrus industry had to wait until 1911–12 for the next good crop.

STREET SCENE
Shown here is downtown Winter Park in 1896, still recovering from the Big Freeze. It shows considerably less activity than there had been prior to the freeze, but since the town was not solely dependent upon the citrus industry, it survived while many other towns did not. *Courtesy of the Florida Photographic Collection.*

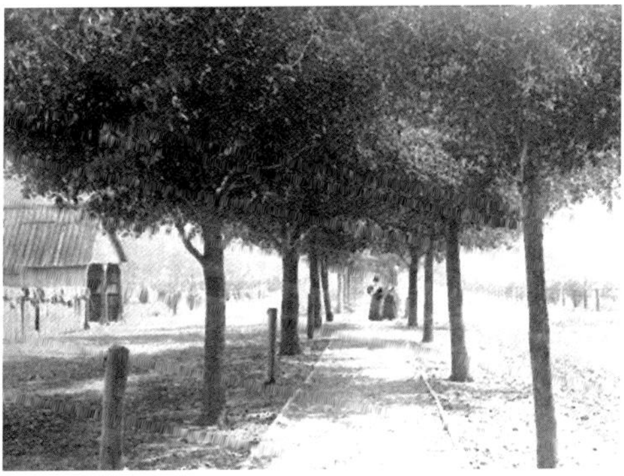

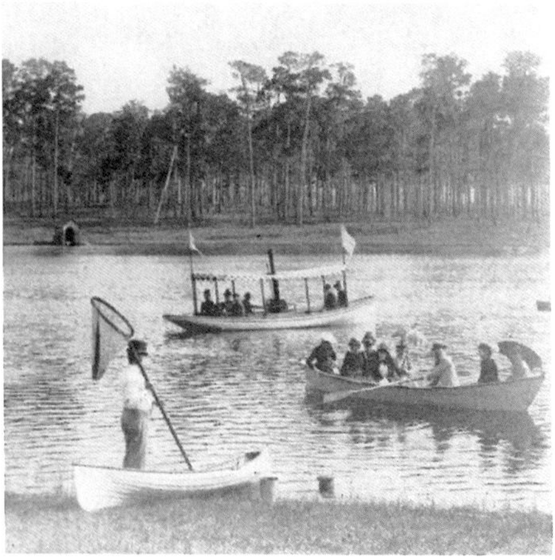

LAKE OSCEOLA
Steamers, canoes, sailboats and rowboats were extremely popular with tourists during the winter hotel season. While their neighbors back home were waiting for lakes and rivers to thaw out, those who could afford to stay at the Seminole Hotel or other lodgings were able to enjoy Central Florida's recreational opportunities. *Courtesy of the Florida Photographic Collection.*

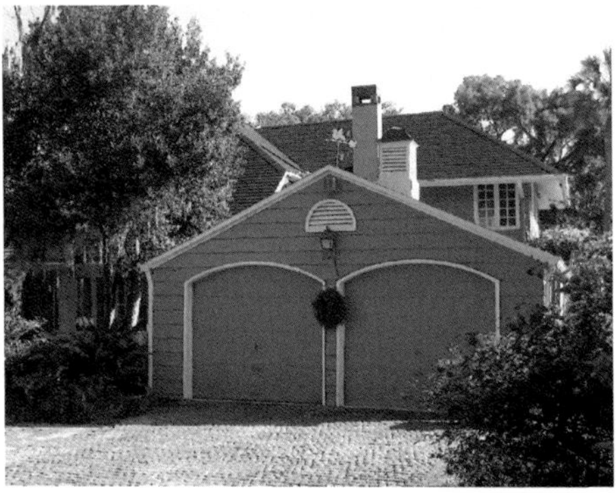

GIBBS-GREENE COTTAGE
Shown here is one of the homes erected on the former Seminole Hotel site. Harley B. Gibbs built it at 242 Chase Avenue, and it was purchased by W.D. Freeman in 1919. It was inherited by Billie Freeman, the wife of Ray Greene, a local real estate salesman and a Rollins faculty member. *Photo by Steve Rajtar.*

The 1900s

SEMINOLE HOTEL FIRE

The hotel burned to the ground on September 18, 1902. The fire began in the kitchen annex while it was still closed for the summer, and although a caretaker was present, he did not know how to use the fire hoses. During its operation, the Seminole attracted statesmen and celebrities, including two U.S. presidents and author Harriet Beecher Stowe. The railroad tracks were removed from New England Avenue in 1903. In 1906, Reverend G.D. Simon Jr. bought the property, including the ruins, that extended to the brook connecting Lakes Osceola and Virginia.

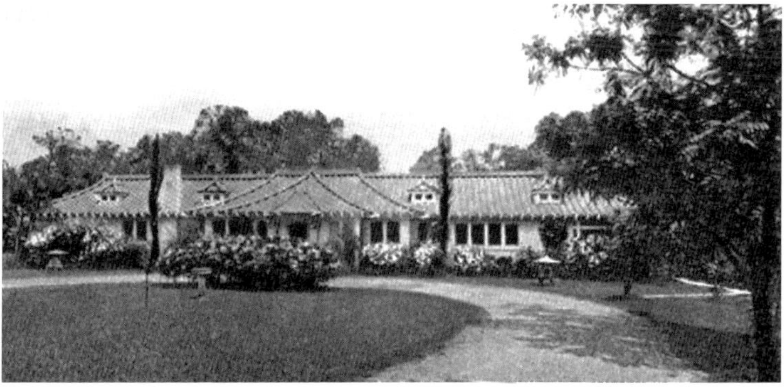

BACHELLER HOUSE
Previously, this lot was the site of Gate o' the Isles, the cottage of A. Irving Bacheller, shown in this image from the 1920s. He was a novelist, beginning with his 1892 book, *The Master of Silence*. He was best known for *Eben Holden*, which was the fourth bestselling novel in the country during 1900. *Courtesy of the Florida Photographic Collection.*

LAKEMONT DAIRY

Clara B. Ward bought a cow so her children would have milk. Milk from a second cow was shared with neighbors and friends. That formed the nucleus of the Lakemont Dairy located along Lakemont Avenue beginning in 1906 when the Wards had four cows and a horse-drawn milk delivery wagon. The Wards continued to expand and modernize their operation until 1952, when they sold their milk routes to T.G. Lee and continued to produce milk for that company. The original land was sold in 1957 and the herd was moved elsewhere.

PALM CEMETERY

Loring Chase donated about three acres at 301 West Webster Avenue in 1906 as a town burial ground for white people. Fourteen more acres were added later. Many prominent residents

INTERLACHEN AVENUE
Today's Interlachen is an avenue of churches, magnificent homes and condominiums. When this photo appeared on a postcard that was mailed in 1906, what dominated the narrow dirt road was a line of tall live oaks and a few cottages. *Courtesy of the Florida Photographic Collection.*

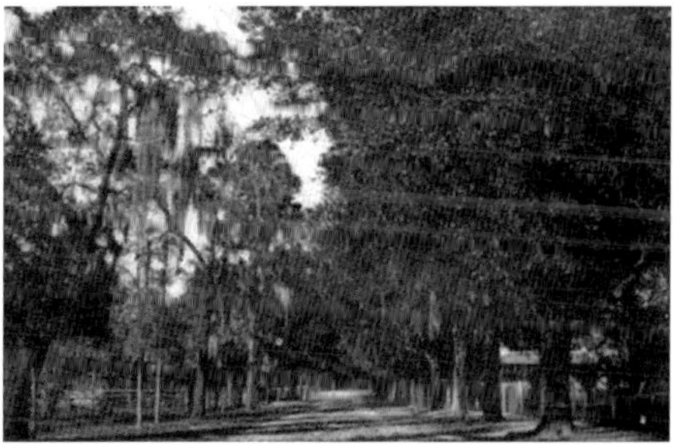

are buried there, including Loring Chase, Charles and Harold Ward, Reuben Foley, Herbert Barnum, Richard Batchelor, Edward Keezel, Charles Coffin, Eulalie Grover, Carl Galloway and William Temple.

BOARD OF TRADE

The Village Improvement Association became the Board of Trade in 1909. The reorganized association's officers included President William Temple and Vice-president George L. Dyer. Its early projects included building a dock at the end of Ollie Avenue, maintaining Palm Cemetery starting in 1917 and providing metal street signs. Since 1923, it has been known as the Winter Park Chamber of Commerce. One of its first actions under that name was the adoption of the city slogan, "City of Trees."

The 1910s

CENTRAL PARK

When Chase and Chapman founded Winter Park in 1881, the central portion was covered with orange trees. They were cut down in 1894 to create a green space around the train station. Charles Morse deeded the adjacent park to the city in 1906, with the stipulation that it must always remain a park.

At the north end of the park is a memorial to Eve Proctor Morrill, who helped create the Park Avenue shopping area in the 1950s and 1960s. Nearby is the 1982 bandstand donated by

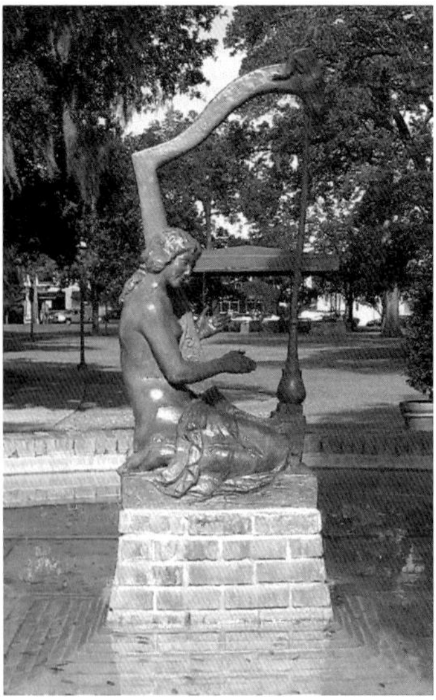

CENTRAL PARK FOUNTAIN
This Central Park landmark features a sculpture by Albin Polasek, which was placed in its center in 1984. When water flows upward through the body of the sculpted harp and down through a row of holes, it creates the illusion of harp strings. *Photo by Steve Rajtar.*

the Rotary Club and a canopy given by Southeast Bank. In the park is a monument to Charles Morse and a memorial fountain to honor those who died in World War I (later rededicated to include other wars).

SECOND SEMINOLE HOTEL

A second Seminole Hotel was built at the foot of Webster Avenue in 1912. The second Seminole Hotel was smaller than the original, having eighty-two rooms. It was managed by Reuben Foley from 1913 until he died in 1927, when he was succeeded by his son John S. Foley. One of the hotel's most famous guests was President Calvin Coolidge, who visited there in 1929. The hotel and its land were sold for $250,000 in 1970 and the building was replaced by homes along Kiwi Circle.

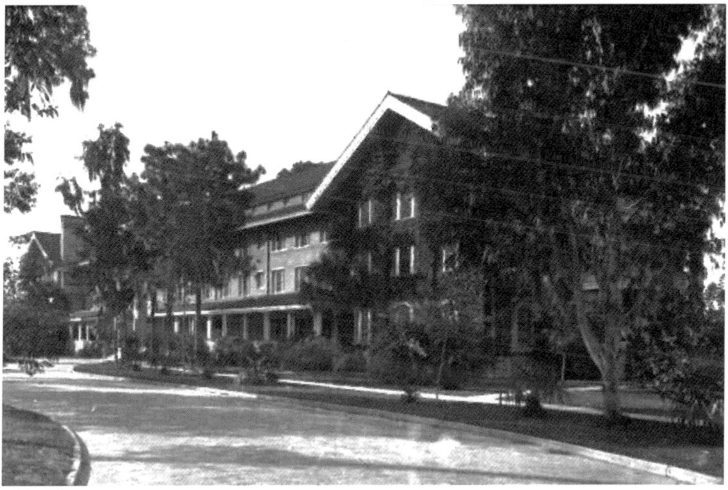

SECOND SEMINOLE HOTEL
Ten years after the first Seminole Hotel burned down along the south shore of Lake Osceola, a new hotel was built along the northwest shore. Called the "New Seminole" or "Second Seminole" or just the "Seminole," it bore no resemblance to the original one except for the name. *Courtesy of the Florida Photographic Collection.*

TELEPHONE COMPANY

Brothers B.A. and Carl H. Galloway obtained a franchise for the Winter Park Telephone Exchange in 1912. Its first phone was installed in Trovillion's Grove. It was not the first in the city, however, as J.B. Steinmetz, in 1901, had connected his home in Clay Springs with Rollins College to keep in touch with his daughter there. In 1913, Winter Park's exchange was combined with the Galloways' exchange in Maitland to form the Winter Park Telephone Company. Carl moved the business to Winter Park in 1914, and in 1918 he laid the town's first underground telephone cable. In 1979, the company merged with the United Telephone Company and subsequently became part of Sprint.

FIRST BAPTIST CHURCH OF WINTER PARK

Thirteen members of the First Baptist Church of Orlando met at the home of R.L. Betts in 1913 and organized the First Baptist Church of Winter Park. Charter members Mr. and Mrs. Jerry A. Trovillion donated land, and construction began in August that same year. The present sanctuary at 1021 North New York Avenue was built in 1960–61.

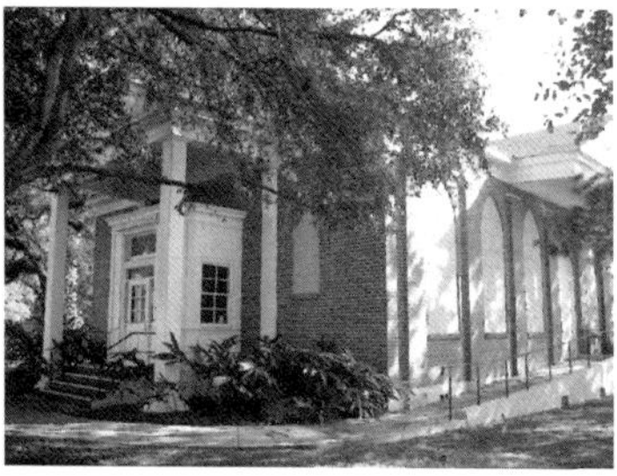

FIRST BAPTIST CHURCH
The First Baptist Church of Winter Park built a small sanctuary at the intersection of Interlachen and Comstock Avenues. In 1961, that property was conveyed to the college, which converted it into the Fred Stone Theatre when the theatre's previous home across the street could no longer be used. *Photo by Steve Rajtar.*

WOMAN'S CLUB

The Woman's Club of Winter Park was formed by sixteen women who met in 1915 at Osceola Lodge, the home of Mrs. Charles Morse. Their clubhouse was built on South Interlachen Avenue for a cost of $40,000 on a site that, until 1912, had included the tee for a hole on a golf course built by Charles Morse. The course extended south to Lake Virginia and west to New York Avenue. Sheep were used to keep its grass under control.

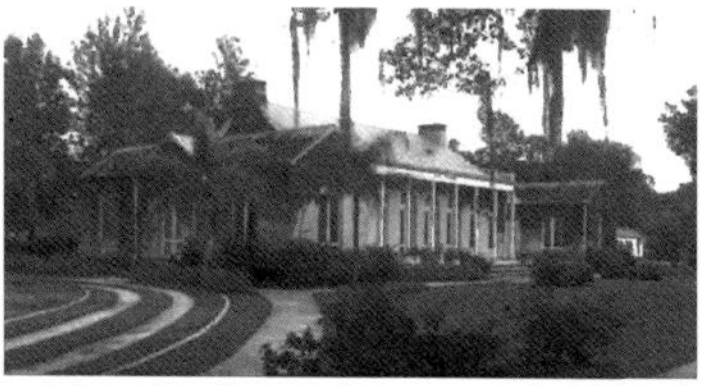

WOMAN'S CLUB
Shown here is the clubhouse of the Woman's Club of Winter Park. Construction of the building was completed in December 1920 and the club hosted its first meeting on January 21, 1921. The building was added to the National Register of Historic Places in 1995. *Courtesy of the Florida Photographic Collection.*

FIRE DEPARTMENT

In 1915, Fire Chief E.R. Favor expanded the fire department by the acquisition of a fire wagon pulled by a single horse. In the wagon were five hundred feet of hose and a ladder. The following year, the horse was replaced by a motorized vehicle. Firefighters were still volunteers and remained so until the early 1950s.

TEMPLE ORANGE

William C. Temple of Pittsburgh moved to Winter Park in 1898. He helped form the Florida Citrus Exchange in 1909 and was its head in 1915, when Louis Hakes made a discovery at the grove adjacent to his home, east of downtown.

Hakes noticed an unusual fruit on a tree along his driveway and showed it to Temple, who had a sample sent to D.C. Gillett of Tampa. Gillett concluded that the strange fruit was a cross between an orange and a tangerine, and he budded thousands of new trees from it. So that Gillett's Buckeye Nursery could obtain a patent for the new fruit, it needed a name. Temple suggested "the Winter Park hybrid," but the name chosen was the Temple orange, recommended by *The Florida Grower* magazine because of the part that William Temple played in the process.

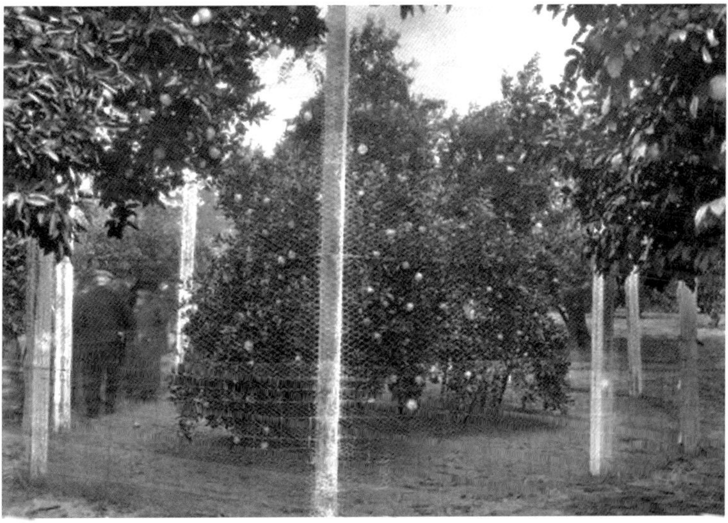

TEMPLE ORANGE TREE

The first tree recognized to bear Temple oranges was sold to the Buckeye Nurseries of Tampa, which erected a padlocked fence around it. It has been estimated that the single tree shown in this 1920 photo was the ancestor of more than seven million descendant trees. *Courtesy of the Florida Photographic Collection.*

WORLD WAR I

Local residents became involved in the national military effort shortly after war was declared in 1917. The town hall was used by the National Surgical Dressings Committee for the making of bandages to be sent overseas. The Country Club Auxiliary also made dressings for wounded soldiers. The country club golf course was converted into pastureland for sheep and goats. A Winter Park Branch of the National Home Guard was organized.

The 1920s

CHARLES MORSE

Charles H. Morse of Chicago retired to Winter Park in 1905 and bought most of what had been Osceola. He built his home and kept 150 acres undeveloped as a refuge from the hustle and bustle of the city. A road was laid out through the property in 1916, and in 1936, Morse named it Genius Drive after his daughter and son-in-law, Elizabeth and Richard Genius.

Until recently, Genius Drive was managed by the Winter Park Land Company, which permitted the public to drive along the road around Lake Mizell and enjoy the solitude, interrupted only by the calls of more than a hundred wild peacocks. Public access to the area was limited beginning in 1987. The land, which stretches south to Glenridge Way, is now the subject of upscale residential development.

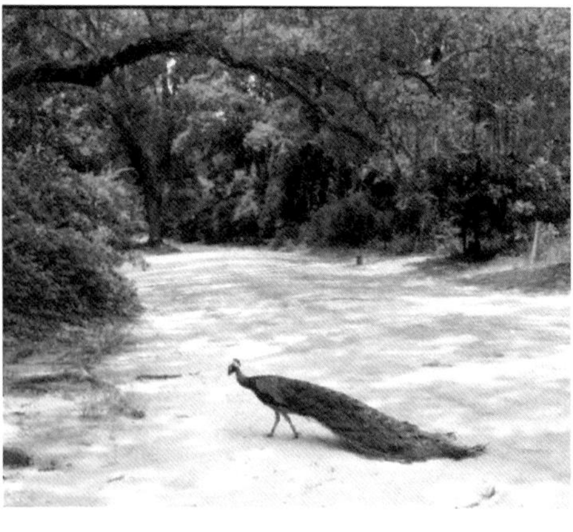

GENIUS DRIVE
Hugh and Jeannette McKean acquired a pair of peacocks in 1950, intending to have them live in their front yard along Interlachen Avenue. Shortly thereafter, they learned that peacocks are very noisy, and they moved them to a less-populated area along Genius Drive. *Courtesy of the Florida Photographic Collection.*

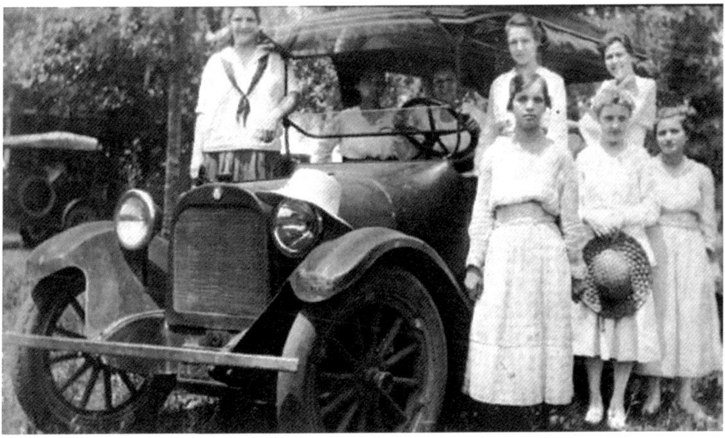

ON THE WAY TO Y CAMP
The popular Y camp held on the Rollins College campus under the supervision of the Women's Christian Temperance Union attracted participants from distant locations. Shown here in about 1920 are some who participated in the camp. They rode to Rollins from Tampa in this car driven by one of their cousins. *Courtesy of the Florida Photographic Collection.*

Y CAMP

During the 1920s, a popular summer activity was the Y Camp operated by the Women's Christian Temperance Union. It was set up for girls, but all female members of the WCTU were welcome to participate. Chase Hall, Cloverleaf Cottage, athletic facilities and other portions of the Rollins campus provided a setting for classes and "character talks" led by evangelists.

WINTER PARK GARDEN CLUB

The Garden Committee of the Woman's Club of Winter Park was organized by Grace O. Edwards in 1922, and in 1923 it became a separate organization called the Winter Park Garden Club. It was one of the four charter members of the Florida Federation of Garden Clubs in 1925.

ST. MARGARET MARY CATHOLIC CHURCH

The first Roman Catholic Mass in Winter Park was celebrated in about 1900 at the home of John H. LaMontagne. Before that, local Catholics traveled to Orlando to attend church. In 1924, a cornerstone for a new church was laid at the corner of Knowles and Canton Avenues on October 17, the feast day of Saint Margaret Mary of Alacoque.

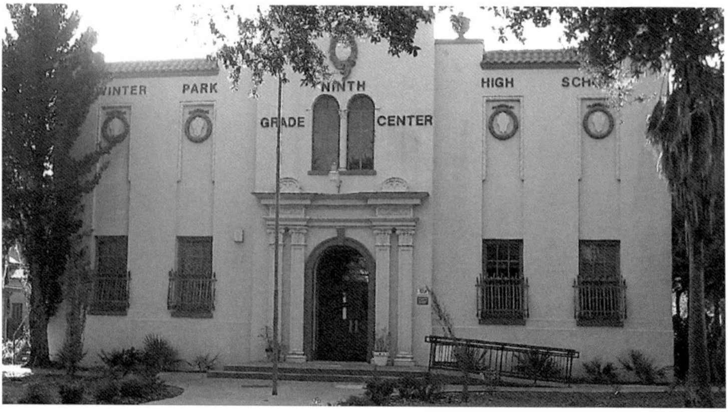

High School
Winter Park High School opened in 1926 in this building designed by Howard M. Reynolds. In the 1970s, most of the students moved to a new facility to the east and this became a ninth-grade center. *Photo by Steve Rajtar.*

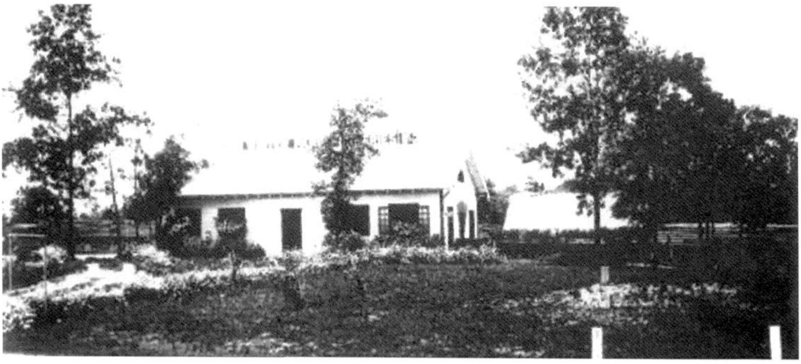

Ferneries
In the 1920s, Hibbard Casselberry owned a small Park Avenue floral shop. He opened a fern-growing business known as Winter Park Ferneries, supplying ferns at a much lower price than was charged by Northern growers. He also acquired three thousand acres north of Winter Park, and during the 1940s he developed this land as the city of Casselberry. *Courtesy of the Florida Photographic Collection.*

The completed sanctuary was officially dedicated in 1927, and the church received its first resident pastor in 1947. The present church at 526 North Park Avenue, designed by Stiekle International Architects, was dedicated in 1969.

Athletic Field

James Harper and Forney Shepherd deeded land to the city in 1926 along Orange Avenue for the construction of a municipal athletic field. The grandstand of the Harper-Shepherd Recreation Park cost $5,000 and was completed in 1927. In 1984, the new Harold Alfond Stadium on the site was dedicated and named for a major benefactor.

EULALIE GROVER

Eulalie Osgood Grover moved to Winter Park in 1926 and is remembered for the children's books she authored, especially the Sunbonnet Babies series including *The Sunbonnet Babies' Primer*. She began writing the books in 1902 and they were used by second- and third-grade teachers of reading and geography.

JAMES GAMBLE ROGERS II

In 1915, James Gamble Rogers II of Chicago moved to Daytona Beach and later studied art and architecture at Dartmouth. He was named for his uncle, James Gamble Rogers. He joined the architectural practice of his father, John Arthur Rogers, and upon John's death in 1928, James opened his own practice in Winter Park.

Desiring a home on the Isle of Sicily, a twelve-acre parcel of land on the eastern side of Lake Maitland, Rogers set out a

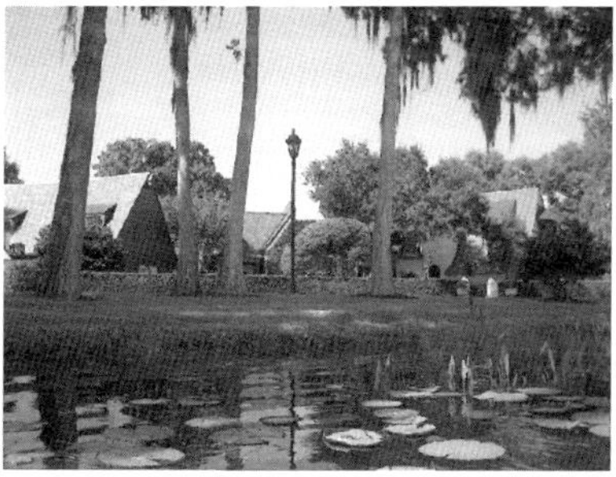

ISLE OF SICILY

Connected to the eastern shore of Lake Maitland is a development of exclusive homes. Shown here from the water is a portion of one, Four Winds, the home James Gamble Rogers II designed for himself. It was substantially rebuilt in 1992, but it retains many of the original elements such as the unusual chimney tops. *Photo by Steve Rajtar.*

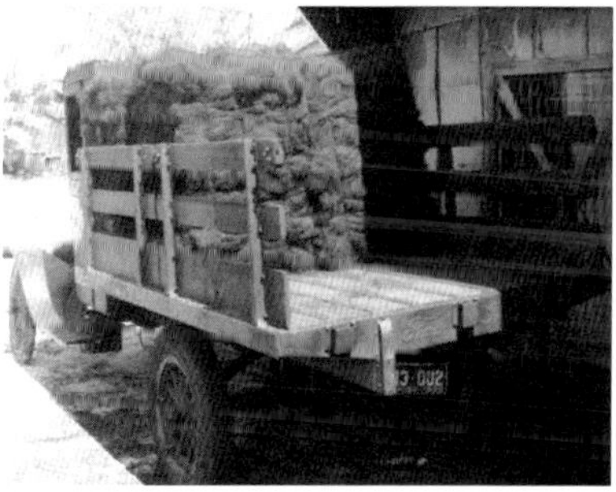

SPANISH MOSS

Ever present is Spanish moss, a plant that hangs from trees and resembles long, gray beards. At times it has been used in the manufacture of mattresses and other furniture. In this 1930 photo, a load of moss is ready to be taken to a factory and turned into stuffing. *Courtesy of the Florida Photographic Collection.*

dozen homesites in exchange for his receiving the first lot (with an address of 3 Isle of Sicily). On it, he built the 1,800-square-foot French Provincial–style Four Winds at a cost of $13,000 and lived in it until 1949. A subsequent owner enlarged it to nearly 9,500 square feet. After World War II, his firm became the official architects of Rollins College.

The 1930s

UNIVERSITY CLUB

The club was organized in 1934 at the chamber of commerce building by Kenyon L. Butterfield, a retired president of the University of Massachusetts. It met there, and in the Alabama Hotel and the country club building, until 1948, when the present clubhouse designed by James Gamble Rogers II opened at 841 North Park Avenue.

The first bylaws required members to hold a degree from a college or university, or to have graduated from the U.S. Military or Naval Academies. Others could get in by special vote, but non-degree holders were not permitted to constitute more than 10 percent of the club.

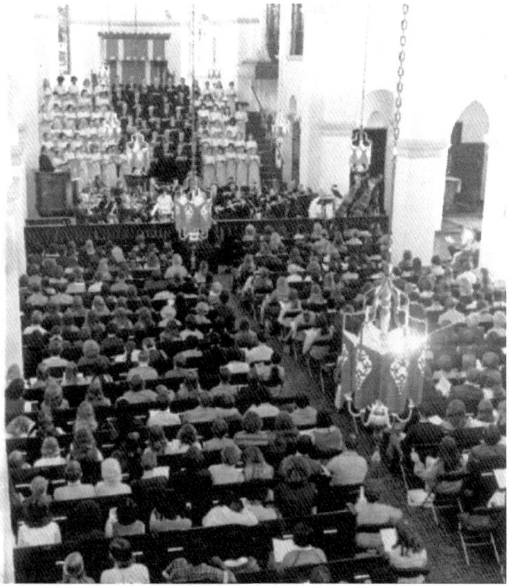

BACH FESTIVAL
The Bach Festival Society of Winter Park was founded in 1935 to commemorate the 250th birthday of Johann Sebastian Bach. From then until 1950, Isabelle Sprague-Smith led the community choir in its presentation of orchestral and choral music for the public. Today, the 160-voice choir presents the music of Bach and other artists at Rollins and other venues. *Courtesy of the Florida Photographic Collection.*

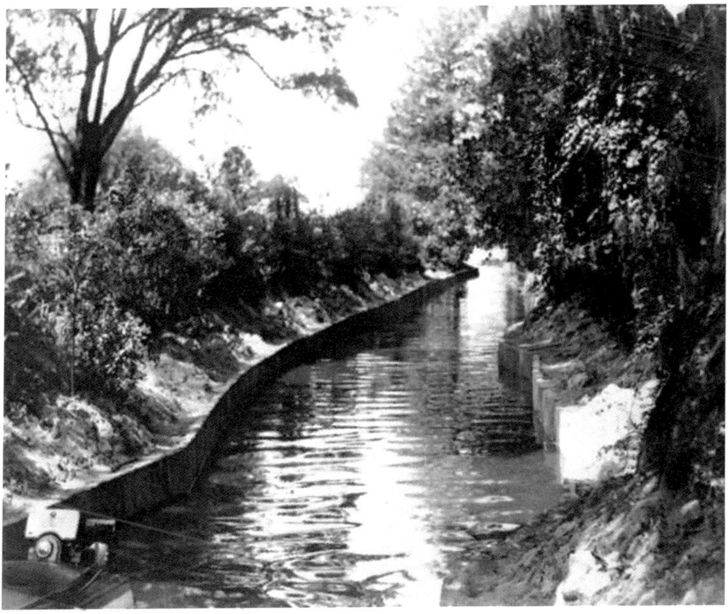

CANALS
During the Great Depression, many were put to work in government programs, often constructing public buildings and other projects. Winter Park's canals were worked on under the auspices of the Federal Emergency Relief Administration (FERA), resulting in wider and deeper channels to allow larger boats. *Courtesy of the Florida Photographic Collection.*

HANNIBAL SQUARE LIBRARY

The Hannibal Square Library organized in 1936, and in 1937 Hannibal Square Associates organized and erected a building on lots donated by the city for that purpose and a park. It was located next to the black elementary school on New England Avenue that had been built in 1927. The Hannibal Square Public Library–Mertie Graham Grover Memorial opened in 1938, became a branch of the Winter Park Library in 1968 and closed in 1979.

MEAD BOTANICAL GARDEN

This fifty-five-acre park at 1300 South Denning Drive includes Howell Creek connecting Lakes Virginia and Sue. It was founded in 1937 by John H. Connery and Edwin G. Grover and was named for Dr. Theodore L. Mead, a horticulturist who settled in Oviedo during the early 1880s.

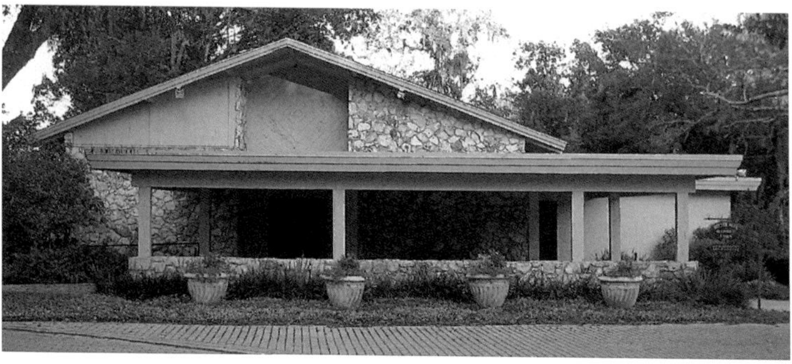

MEAD BOTANICAL GARDEN
This park was dedicated in 1940, including a pair of greenhouses full of orchids. Construction was facilitated by a contribution by the Works Progress Administration (WPA). The city took it over and it has been the meeting place of the Winter Park Garden Club since the 1950s. *Photo by Steve Rajtar.*

The 1940s

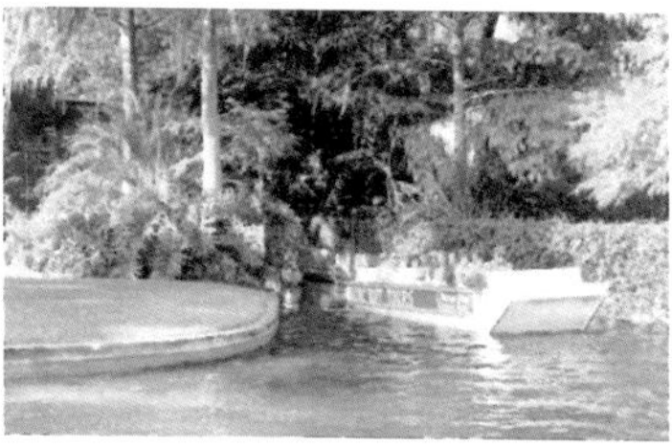

SCENIC BOAT TOUR
Walt Meloon conducted his first official tour through Lakes Osceola, Virginia and Maitland on his twenty-five-passenger boat named *Scenic* on January 1, 1938. Since then, the Scenic Boat Tour has taken visitors through the lakes and canals that give the area the nickname of "Venice of America." *Courtesy of the Florida Photographic Collection.*

MORSE MUSEUM OF AMERICAN ART

This museum was founded by Jeannette Genius McKean in 1942 as a part of the college, in memory of her grandfather, Charles Morse. It has been a separate institution since 1976, owned and operated by the Elizabeth Morse Genius and Charles Hosmer Morse Foundation. It includes late nineteenth- and early twentieth-century American paintings, sculpture and decorative arts, and is best known for the work of Louis Comfort Tiffany.

The Tiffany collection, considered to be the world's most extensive, was assembled in 1955 by the gallery's founder and includes most of the leaded windows personally designed by Tiffany. It also includes his *Electrolier*, a thousand-pound electrified chandelier designed for the 1893 Chicago World Columbian Exposition. The McKeans brought it from the chapel at Tiffany's burned Long Island estate in the 1950s.

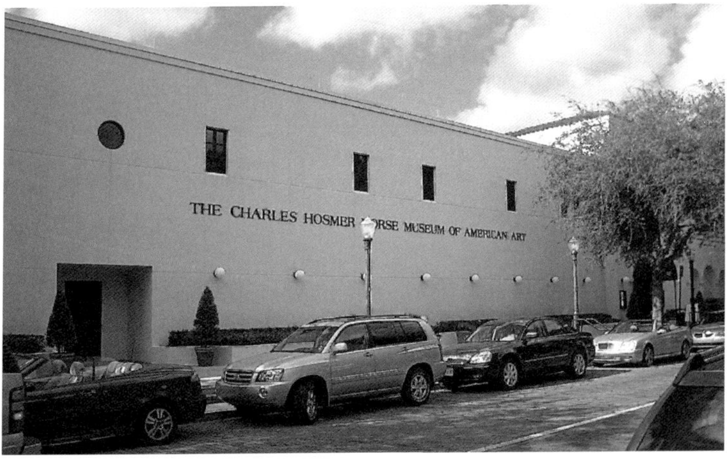

MORSE MUSEUM

Hugh McKean, husband to Jeannette and an art professor at, and president of, Rollins College, was the director of the museum for fifty-three years. It was located at 151 East Welbourne Avenue beginning in 1977, and in 1995 it opened a much larger gallery in the building shown here at 445 North Park Avenue. *Photo by Steve Rajtar.*

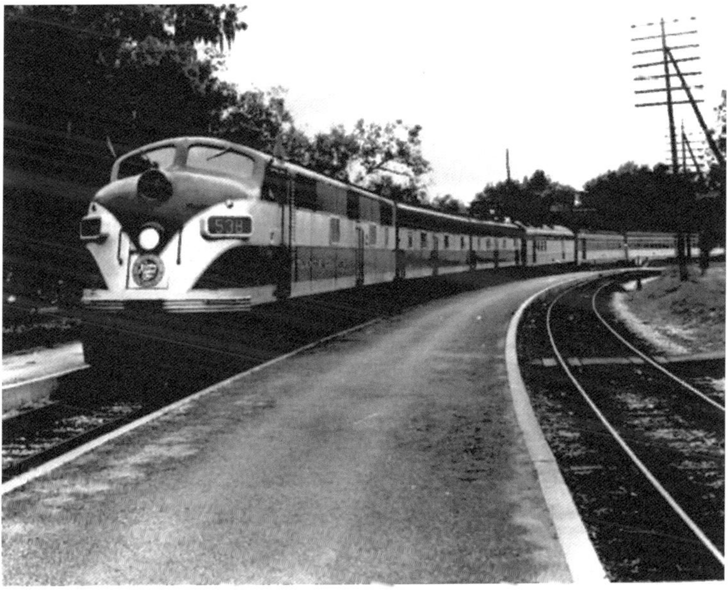

RAILROAD

The railroad depot, located within a block of the downtown shopping area, remains a popular means of transportation. Shown here from the 1940s is the *Champion*, one of the purple, silver and gold Atlantic Coast Line engines, as it pulled up along the embarkation area next to Central Park. *Courtesy of the Florida Photographic Collection.*

Hannibal Square

Although Hannibal Square was officially in Winter Park, there was still the desire by many white residents to keep it separate. An agreement was reached in 1944 by the city and the West Side Civic League to establish and uphold boundaries between the black and white sections. The city bought thirteen lots in the black section to trade with black individuals who had bought lots in the white section.

The 1950s

Winter Park Memorial Hospital

A large parcel at 200 North Lakemont Avenue includes 360 acres purchased by Winter Park Golf Estates Inc., formed by Roland Hotard in the 1920s. On it was built the Aloma Country Club during 1926, including a 6,180-yard golf course and homes. Economic conditions changed and the clubhouse, with its distinctive three-story tower, was allowed to deteriorate until the 1950s, when it was torn down to make room for the Winter Park Memorial Hospital chartered in 1951 and now a part of Florida Hospital.

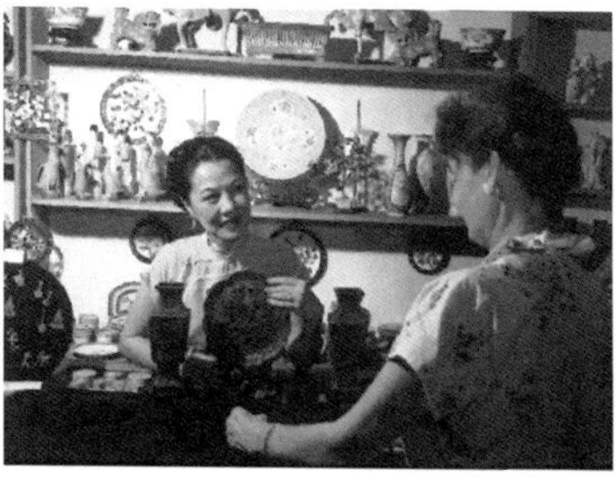

Park Avenue Shops
In the 1950s, Winter Park's reputation as a shopping Mecca grew and attracted both shoppers and unique retailers. Shown here is Soo Yong, a Chinese actress who appeared in Hollywood movies and television shows and did annual winter tours promoting Chinese subjects. Between tours, she assisted her husband in their exclusive Park Avenue Chinese novelty shop, the Jade Lantern. *Courtesy of the Florida Photographic Collection.*

Albin Polasek

While Albin Polasek was the head of the sculpture department at the Chicago Institute of Art in 1914, he had a student named Ruth Sherwood. In 1950, at the age of seventy-one, he came to Winter Park to visit her. He decided to stay, bought land fronting on Lake Osceola and they were married later that year. Within a year, Ruth died. Both are buried in Palm Cemetery.

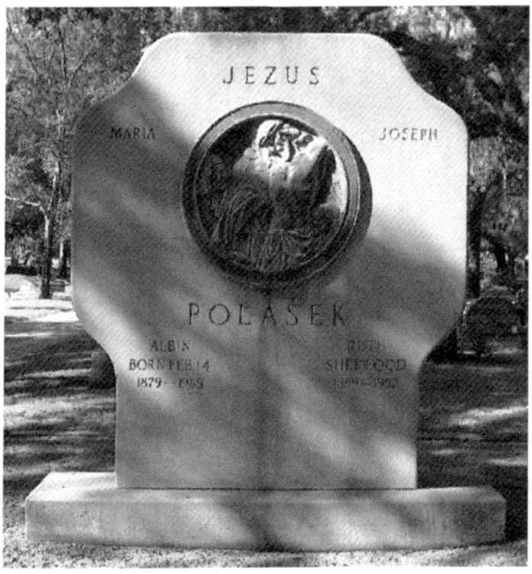

POLASEK MONUMENT
Albin Polasek and his student and wife Ruth Sherwood were both sculptors, so it is fitting that their tombstone should be different from the typical slabs, steles or obelisks of most others interred here. The modified cross sculpture marks their graves in Palm Cemetery. *Photo by Steve Rajtar.*

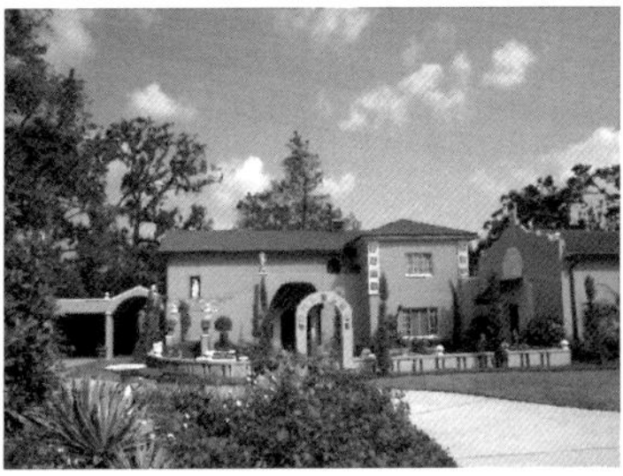

POLASEK HOUSE
The Albin Polasek Foundation preserves the studio-home built by the artist at 633 Osceola Avenue as a memorial museum where his works may be viewed by the public. On the front wall along the sidewalk is *Evoking Memories*, a sample of what can be viewed by entering the facility, which was placed on the National Register of Historic Places in 2000. *Courtesy of the Albin Polasek Foundation, Inc. Photo by Wendy Murray.*

Three works that can be viewed, in addition to those on display at his preserved studio-home, are *Forest Idyll* at the entrance to the city hall, *Man Carving His Own Destiny* on the grounds of the library and *Emily* in a Central Park fountain.

FIRST CHURCH OF CHRIST, SCIENTIST

Thirty Christian Scientists met in November 1952 to consider organizing a Christian Science society. Its first service was held at the University Club later that year. They opened a reading room the following October and bought property at 650 North New York Avenue in 1954.

That same year, the society became the First Church of Christ, Scientist, Winter Park, and the first service in the building designed by James Gamble Rogers II was held on January 4, 1959.

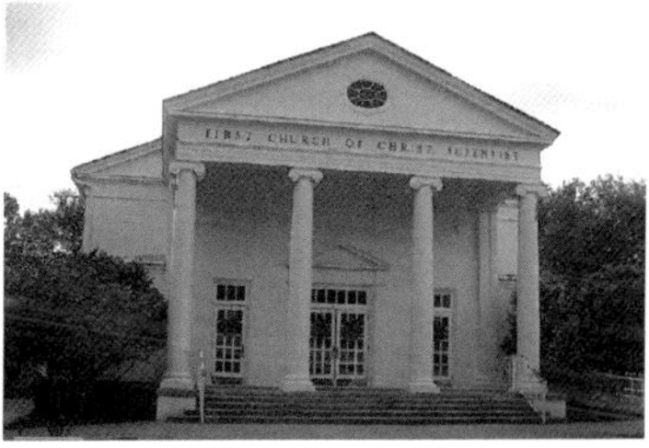

FIRST CHURCH OF CHRIST, SCIENTIST
This large church with a view of the golf course was designed by James Gamble Rogers II. Additions to the building that were completed in early 1985 include a children's room, boardroom facilities, an enlarged Sunday school area and additional parking. *Photo by Steve Rajtar.*

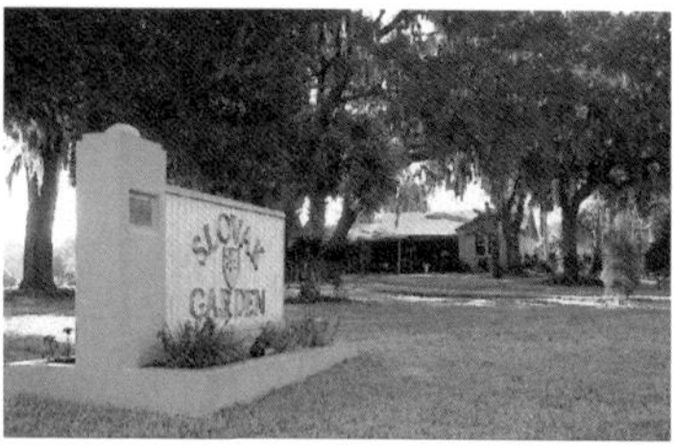

SLOVAK GARDEN
Along Howell Branch Road, well east of downtown, is a large complex of buildings, mostly small, one-story apartments, but it also includes the large Faith Outreach Church. The campus is marked with this sign, bearing a plaque honoring Milan Bêlohlávek. *Photo by Steve Rajtar.*

SLOVAK GARDEN

Slovak Garden was founded in 1952 by Mary and Karol Bêlohlávek as a retirement community and cultural center for American Slovaks in Florida. They opened the facility on forty acres, including a two-bedroom house and a citrus grove. In 1988, the Slovak Garden Library and Museum was established in the memory of the founders and is open to the public at 3110 Howell Branch Road.

WINTER PARK MALL

During the 1950s, the 400,000-square-foot Winter Park Mall opened along Orlando Avenue and became a popular place to shop. On April 6, 1969, the mall made history by being the site of the country's first major fire involving an enclosed mall. Five fire departments brought the blaze under control within four hours. As a result of competition from other malls and Park Avenue shops, the mall was torn down and replaced in 1999 by the outdoor shops of Winter Park Village.

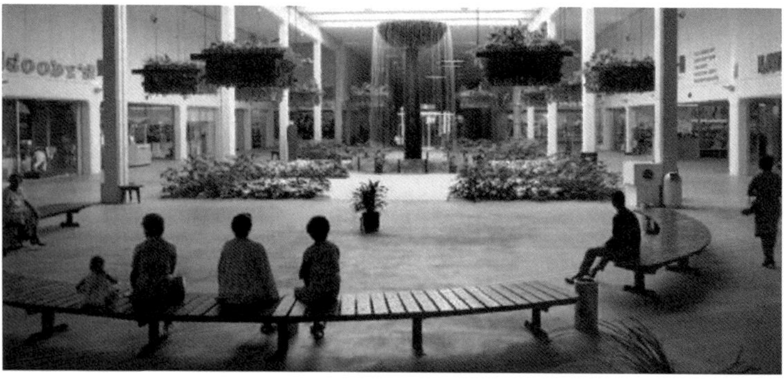

WINTER PARK MALL
The mall had a distinctive appearance, with two tall white towers flanking its main entrance. Indoors was a large fountain (described as a "spilling chalice" and shown in this 1966 photo) and foliage along its air-conditioned hallways connecting the stores and eateries. *Courtesy of the Florida Photographic Collection.*

The 1960s

MORSE BOULEVARD

When this major east–west thoroughfare opened in the 1880s, it ended at the railroad depot. During 1962, the boulevard was extended westward to Orlando Avenue (U.S. 17–92), facilitating access to Orlando and other cities. As part of the extension, the 1913 depot was torn down.

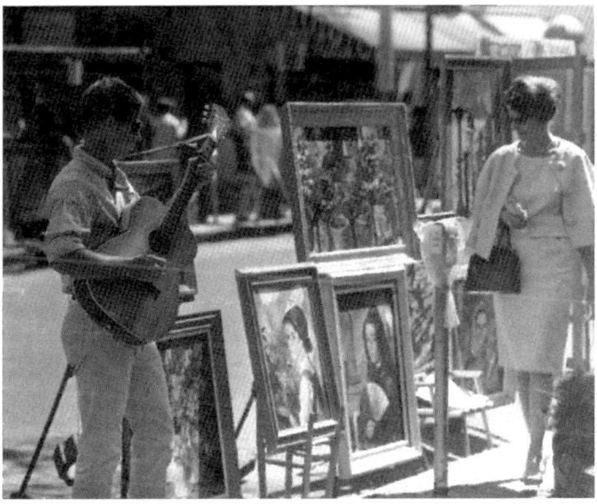

ART FESTIVAL
In one Central Park fountain is Albin Polasek's sculpture, *Emily*, presented to the city in 1984 to commemorate the twenty-fifth anniversary of the Winter Park Sidewalk Art Festival. The annual event attracts more than 250,000 people to view the work of artists and craftsmen. *Courtesy of the Florida Photographic Collection.*

The 1970s

HISTORICAL ASSOCIATION

The Winter Park Historical Association formed in 1974 at a meeting held in the home of Alfred J. Hanna. He and six others established the organization that now operates the Winter Park Historical Museum.

CREALDÉ SCHOOL OF ART

In 1975, William S. Jenkins founded a nonprofit art school to give local artists an affordable studio and a gallery to display their works. The school, located at 600 St. Andrews Boulevard, conducts more than eighty classes in a variety of art forms.

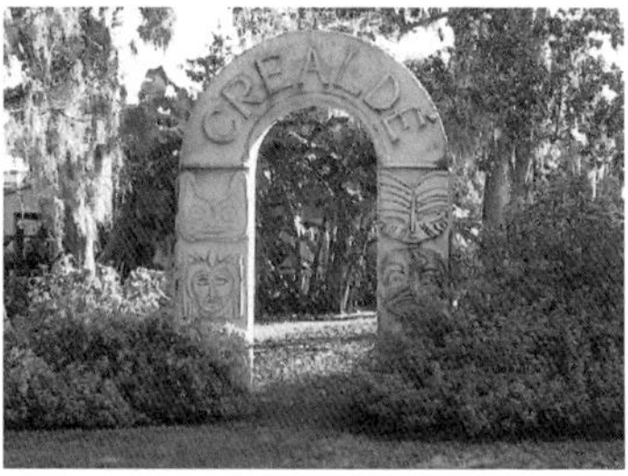

CREALDÉ SCHOOL
Behind the stuccoed Mediterranean buildings used for administration, classes and display is a sculpture garden. One passes through this massive stone arch to a landscaped area for relaxation and contemplation. *Photo by Steve Rajtar.*

The 1980s

WINTER PARK SINKHOLE

After seventy consecutive days in 1981 without rain, a sinkhole swallowed the home of Rosa Mae Owens, several expensive Porsche cars and part of Denning Drive. At 8:00 p.m. on May 8, Owens heard a swishing noise and saw a sycamore tree disappear from her yard. At about noon the following day, her house began to slip into an expanding hole that also swallowed the first of a half-dozen cars that had been parked behind a repair shop. Three commercial structures were damaged.

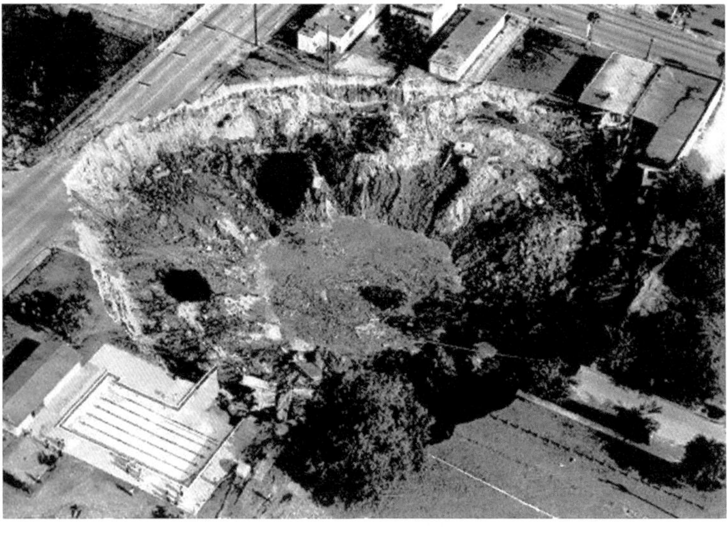

SINKHOLE
In the upper right of this photo is Fairbanks Avenue, along which are retail businesses, including an auto repair shop. A close look at the slope of the huge hole reveals cars that were on their way to the bottom. In the lower left is the city pool, a corner of which collapsed into the sinkhole. *Courtesy of the Florida Photographic Collection.*

It was the largest sinkhole known in the state, and consumed about 250,000 cubic yards of soil. The hole exceeded 335 feet across and 110 feet in depth. After it stabilized and filled with water, it was named Lake Rose. Its size and notoriety were the catalysts for the establishment of the Florida Sinkhole Research Institute at the University of Central Florida. The remains of the house and two Porsches remain beneath the lake.

The 1990s

WINTER PARK HISTORICAL MUSEUM

The museum is located in the Farmers' Market building at 200 West New England Avenue in a renovated 1928 railroad depot and has displays of photographs and memorabilia from the early days. The museum was established in 1995 with ceremonies that included the unveiling of the memorial oak tree and plaque (just to the west of the front door) honoring former mayor Hope Strong Jr. and historical association past presidents John Grass and John Twachtman.

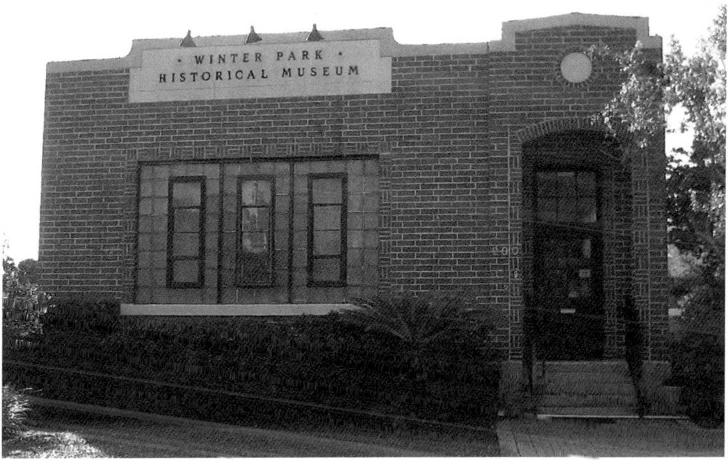

HISTORICAL MUSEUM
In addition to historical displays inside, this facility is the venue for the weekly farmers' market. Growers of fruits and vegetables gather, along with musicians, craftsmen and others, to provide a quaint outdoor shopping experience on Saturday mornings. *Photo by Steve Rajtar.*

The Twenty-first Century

HANNIBAL SQUARE

After a long period of deterioration, buildings in the historical western part of Winter Park were taken down and replaced with shops and restaurants that now attract people from both sides of the city. The Hannibal Square Heritage Center at 642 West New England Avenue opened in 2007 with exhibits on the history and culture of the area and space for classes run by the Crealdé School of Art. Especially interesting are the center's family history research library, historical photographs and oral histories dictated by longtime Hannibal Square residents.

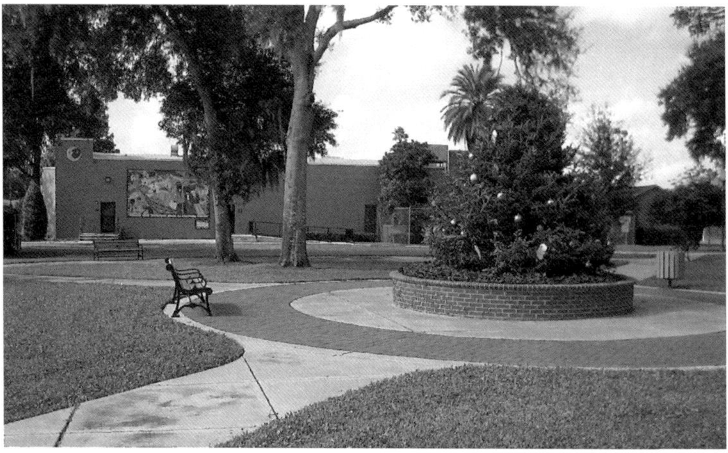

HANNIBAL SQUARE
Many of this neighborhood's old buildings have been replaced with modern restaurants and retail shops. The central area has been beautified by the landscaped Shady Park shown here. In the background can be seen a large mosaic scene designed by local children to represent the early days in Hannibal Square. *Photo by Steve Rajtar.*

Part II

Rollins College

The history of Florida's first college, Rollins College, and the city of Winter Park are interwoven, and the development of both was greatly influenced by the Congregationalist Church with the support of winter residents. Many historians attribute the founding of the college to members of the church, which also established other prestigious institutions such as Harvard, Yale, Dartmouth and Oberlin. Men such as Frederick W. Lyman, who retired to Winter Park from Minneapolis in 1882, and New England Reverend Edward P. Hooker, who had relocated to take over the pulpit of the recently formed Winter Park Congregational Church in 1884, are usually given the credit. However, its origins can actually be traced back to Lucy Cross, a former Wellesley faculty member and principal of the Daytona Institute of Young Women who envisioned a college in Central Florida in 1880.

In December 1883 Cross learned of an upcoming meeting of the Florida Congregational Association to be held in Winter Park and began a proposal to establish a local college. Her paper was presented by the Reverend C.M. Bingham of Daytona. Lyman also had thoughts of a college in Winter Park supported by a sermon presented by Reverend Hooker in January 1884. Hooker again promoted the idea a year later at the second meeting of the association in Orange City, and a decision was made to establish a Congregationalist-supported school. A committee, including Lyman, Hooker, Bingham, Sullivan F. Gale of Jacksonville and R.C. Tremaine of Mt. Dora, was formed to review possible sites in Central Florida.

At a special session of the association held in Mt. Dora on April 15, 1885, it was reported that Jacksonville, Daytona, Interlachen, Orange City, Mt. Dora and Winter Park had expressed the desire to host the college. A $50,000 donation from Alonzo W. Rollins, a New England native who spent winters in Central Florida, cemented the location of the future Rollins College, named for its largest single contributor. The original ten acres of land along Lake Virginia for the campus were given by Winter Park.

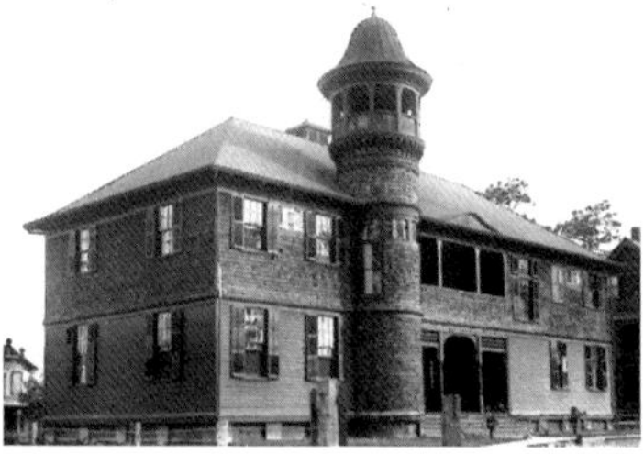

KNOWLES HALL
Knowles Hall was the first building on campus and was completed in less than six months in 1886. Francis Knowles financed the hall, located on ten acres of lakefront property originally intended for a luxury hotel. Knowles Hall was a landmark with a unique bell tower and served as the first classroom building, administrative office, library and chapel. *Courtesy of the Florida Photographic Collection.*

High standards were set for admission due to the belief of the founders in "the New England idea of education, with the New England professor to elucidate it." Expectations were also high, based on the following statement of unknown origin: "It is expected that Rollins College will be to the South what Yale and Harvard have been to the East, and that its fame as an institution of learning will rival theirs."

The initial enrollment of students was small because few public high schools (particularly in the state of Florida) prepared students to pursue a college education. Rollins originally included its own preparatory school, which was customary at that time. The college was coed from the start, offered a four-year degree program and was essentially nonsectarian.

Dr. Edward P. Hooker was named as the first president. The construction of the campus began and was overseen by George Rollins, brother of Alonzo Rollins, in the summer of 1885. A gift from Francis Knowles was used for the construction of Knowles Hall and two dormitories, Pinehurst Cottage for women and Lakeside Cottage for men. The cost of these three buildings was estimated to total $25,000.

Classes began on November 4, 1885, in the Congregational Church and White's Hall on Park Avenue, which was also used as a chapel, library and administrative offices until the opening of the first building on the campus, Knowles Hall, in March 1886. Pinehurst was quickly furnished after Knowles offered to donate money for the construction of a dining hall on the condition that enough money would be raised to cover the Pinehurst furnishings. Pinehurst Cottage is the only remaining building from the original campus—Knowles Hall burned down in 1909 and was subsequently rebuilt, and Lakeside was demolished in 1970. Cloverleaf Cottage for women was built in 1891 on the site where Carnegie Hall is now located. It was moved in 1908 and was used as a women's dorm until its demolition in 1970. A donation from Lyman resulted in the Lyman Gymnasium, which was dedicated in 1891. The gymnasium was moved in 1957 and was lost in a fire in 1974.

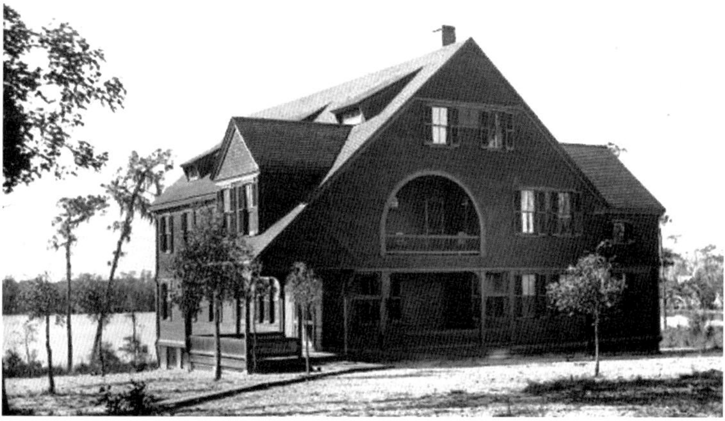

LAKESIDE COTTAGE
The first men's dormitory, Lakeside Cottage, was built in 1886 along with its twin, Pinehurst Cottage for women. While the dormitories were being completed, male students stayed in Deacon Larrabee's house and female students stayed in the Ward Cottage. *Courtesy of the Florida Photographic Collection.*

In addition to the construction of the first buildings, there were several other items of note during Hooker's presidency. Rail service between Orlando and Winter Park was established in 1889 and was affectionately known as the "Dinky Line," which provided a convenient link between the college and local area students. Enrollment was affected by a yellow fever epidemic in 1888 that delayed the opening of the fall term that year, but the student population rebounded within the next two years.

After Hooker retired in 1892 due to ill health, Rollins had two interim presidents, John H. Ford and Charles G. Fairchild. George M. Ward followed as president in 1895. Ward, an ordained Congregationalist minister from Massachusetts, had impressive credentials, including two years at Harvard and degrees from Dartmouth, Boston University and Andover Theological Seminary. This was a particularly difficult period following the Big Freeze of 1894–95 that had virtually devastated Florida, particularly the citrus industry. Ward's abilities, contacts and personality were vital to promote the growth of the college, maintain and attract supporters and to raise funds for operating expenses. He resigned to a reluctant board of trustees in 1902.

William F. Blackman, a Yale sociology professor, became the next president and served from 1902 until 1915. He was an Oberlin graduate with a doctorate degree from Cornell. During Blackman's inauguration, Dr. D.K. Pearson of Chicago offered $50,000 to the board of trustees if an additional $150,000 could be raised within a year for a permanent endowment. Donations exceeded $200,000 and Blackman considered Pearson to be the second founder of

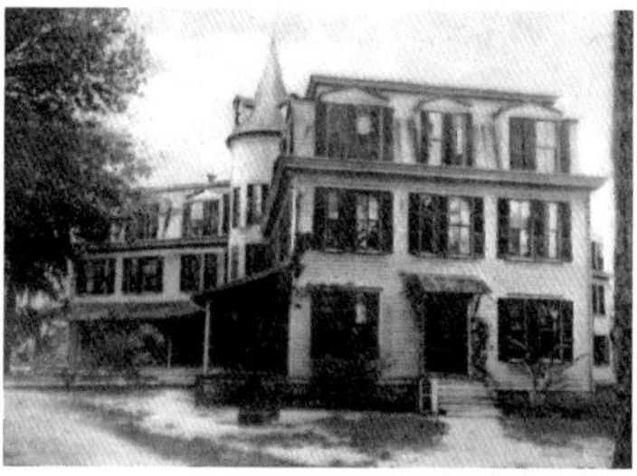

CLOVERLEAF COTTAGE
In 1891, donations from a group of friends of the college were used to construct Cloverleaf Cottage, the largest building on campus at that time. An 1895 editorial in *The Sandspur* suggested the name Cloverleaf because of its three-sided design. *Courtesy of the Florida Photographic Collection.*

the college for establishing the endowment fund.

Part of the fund was presented by Charles Morse and William Temple in the form of the renovated Rogers House, which was renamed the Seminole Inn. The Sparrell House was also donated that year by A.E. Sparrell and was used as a women's dorm.

In later years, it had many uses including living space for Rollins presidents. In 1967, it was demolished and replaced by the Bush Science Center. The growth of the campus took a westward direction in 1909 with the relocation of Cloverleaf Cottage and the dining hall toward Lake Virginia to make room for the Carnegie Library and Chase Hall.

Health issues led to the resignation of Dr. Blackman during the board of trustees' thirtieth annual meeting in 1915. Ward stepped in for two years and was succeeded by Calvin H. French, who served as president from 1917 until 1919. Ward again assumed the presidency, and under his guidance, a fundraising campaign increased the endowment funds to more than $600,000. The trustees made the decision to discontinue the prep school and focus exclusively on the collegiate level of education. Dean R.J. Sprague served as the acting president in 1922–24, followed by William C. Weir, who took over the presidency for the next year until the election of Hamilton Holt in 1925.

Holt graduated from Yale and did postgraduate work at Columbia toward a doctorate, but he never completed his doctoral thesis. Instead, he chose to work at the family-owned-and-established *Independent*, a nationally known journal where he held many positions including managing editor. He was a proponent of reform and founded the League to Enforce Peace, actively supporting the country's membership in the League of Nations.

Holt's progressive views extended into his presidency, establishing Rollins as one of the most experimental and innovative institutions in the nation. Holt's Conference Plan did away with the traditional lecture system, encouraging teachers and students to exchange views around a conference table, a practice still in use today. In this nurturing environment, local

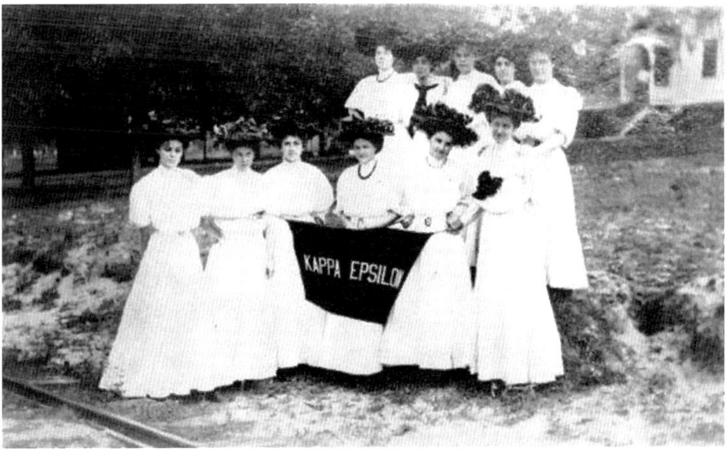

KAPPA EPSILON WOMEN

Rollins was one of the first American colleges to admit both men and women. In 1890, Clara L. Guild became the first person to earn a bachelor's degree in the state of Florida. Kappa Epsilon was one of the earliest sororities on campus and was active from 1903 until 1932. *Courtesy of the Florida Photographic Collection.*

radio station WDBO had its beginnings as a classroom project in 1924 in a small campus building.

During Holt's presidency, the school achieved national recognition and welcomed many notables, including Justice William O. Douglas, Edward R. Murrow and Presidents Roosevelt and Truman. In 1931, the acclaimed John Dewey chaired the national Curriculum Conference held on the campus, and many of the recommendations were applied to the curriculum in the fall, prompting Sinclair Lewis to make mention of Rollins in his acceptance speech for the Nobel Prize in literature. Holt had a major impact on the educational direction of the school and was influential in the direction of its architecture. He also created the Rollins Walk of Fame, which was dedicated in 1929.

Holt remained in office until 1949 and was followed by Paul Wagner, a former Bell & Howell executive who unsuccessfully attempted to introduce impersonal audio-visual techniques into the school's teaching methods. He then worsened matters while attempting to resolve the financial deficit left by Holt due to a decline in enrollment attributed to the draft. Wagner fired nineteen faculty members with the approval of the board of trustees, an act that produced a huge uproar within the college community, including marches and demonstrations. The board had no choice but to ask for his resignation.

Wagner's troubled presidency was followed by the immediate appointment of art professor Hugh F. McKean, who exerted a calming presence during his term of office from 1951–69. He

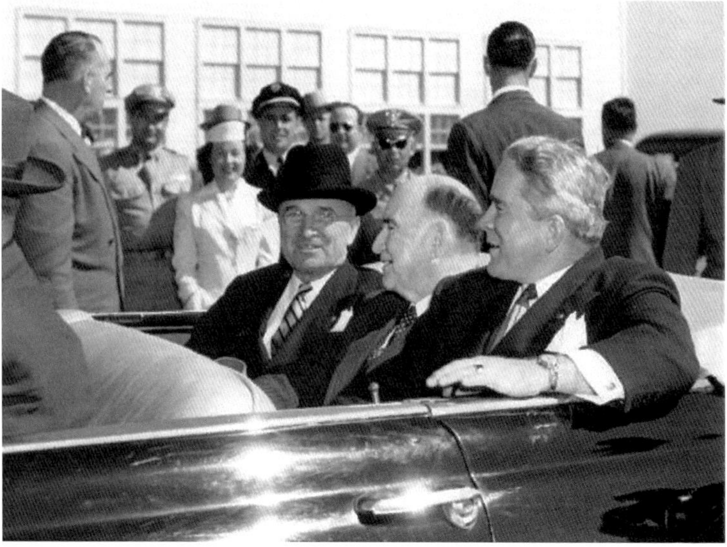

HAMILTON HOLT

During Hamilton Holt's presidency, Rollins hosted many famous figures. In 1949, Holt accompanied President Harry Truman (left) and Florida Governor Fuller Warren (right) for the dedication of the Andrews Causeway, located along Mills Avenue just south of Winter Park. *Courtesy of the Florida Photographic Collection.*

was the first Rollins graduate to assume the presidency, having earned his bachelor's degree there (he was a founding member of the campus fraternity X-Club). He continued his graduate work in New England and abroad and earned his master's degree from Williams College, joining the Rollins faculty in 1932 with a three-year interruption to serve in World War II.

McKean was married to Jeannette Morse Genius, who made substantial contributions to the development of Winter Park and the campus, including the construction of McKean Hall and Elizabeth Hall. She was considered to be the first lady of Rollins and was nicknamed Mrs. Winter Park. She and Hugh founded the Morse Gallery of Art, which became the Charles Hosmer Morse Museum of American Art. Hugh served as its director from its founding in 1942 until 1995.

During McKean's tenure as president, there was significant growth and advancement as the number of faculty members with PhDs doubled, as did the student body. The endowment quadrupled, the curriculum was strengthened and expanded to include the honors degree program, the Hamilton Holt School of Business opened and the soccer program was started.

Several buildings were initially developed or completed during this period, including the Bush Science Center, the Enyart-Alumni Field House, the Art Center and Crummer Hall. The tradition of Fox Day began in 1956, in which a fox statue was placed in the horseshoe (the main campus commons area) by the president, giving students an unexpected day off. In addition to serving on several philanthropic boards, McKean was devoted to making art accessible in Central Florida. He earned a number of honorary degrees and was considered to be the preeminent authority on Tiffany art. He was elected as the first chairman of the board of the local public broadcasting station WMFE, which recently dedicated its facilities in his memory.

Jack B. Critchfield earned his graduate degrees from the University of Pittsburgh and left a position in administration there to serve as the next president in 1969. He was instrumental in establishing environmental and interdisciplinary studies, criminal justice programs and bolstered ties to the local business community. He surprisingly departed the field of education to become the president of the Winter Park Telephone Company in 1978.

The year-long search by the board of trustees for the next president resulted in the appointment of Thaddeus Seymour in 1978. He studied at Princeton, the University of California and the University of North Carolina. Seymour was a scholar with extensive administrative experience—he went on to teach

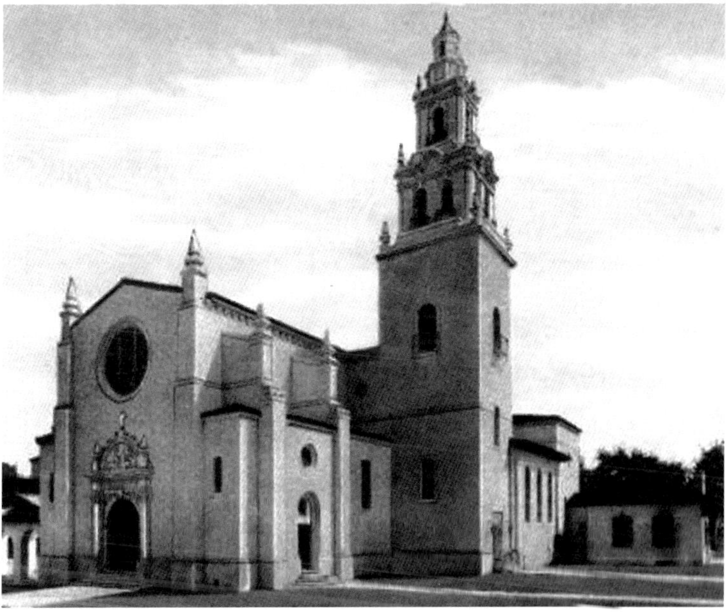

KNOWLES MEMORIAL CHAPEL

The bell in the Knowles Memorial Chapel has historical significance. It was the same bell that rang on November 4, 1885, in the Congregational Church signifying the opening of Rollins College. It was installed in this tower in 1956. *Courtesy of the Florida Photographic Collection.*

at Dartmouth and served as its dean for ten years. Under his leadership, the endowment fund was expanded and changes that are still in effect today were made in the curriculum based on a study by the renowned educator D.S. Bloom.

Seymour presided over the college's centennial celebration and the dedication of the Olin Library in 1985. He remained in office until 1990. Chris Miller, one of the screenwriters of the movie *Animal House* and a former Dartmouth student, claims to have based the character of Dean Wormer on a combination of Richard Nixon and Thaddeus Seymour.

Rita Bornstein became the first female president of Rollins in 1990. She earned her undergraduate and master's degrees from Florida Atlantic University and her doctorate from the University of Miami, where she went on to hold the post of vice-president. Her distinguished career in education included one of the largest fundraising campaigns in the history of higher education at Miami. She conducted The Campaign for Rollins, which helped to quintuple the endowment fund.

A national educational conference held on the campus in 1997 helped reaffirm Rollins as a leader in liberal education. Bornstein raised the standards for faculty, staff and students, as well as the school's national rankings on the list of "America's Best Colleges" from *U.S. News & World Report*. At the end of her presidency in 2004, she was chosen as the Citizen of the Decade by the Winter Park Chamber of Commerce.

The current president, Lewis M. Duncan, was selected in 2004. He received his undergraduate and graduate degrees from Rice University, was an engineering dean at Dartmouth and a provost and senior vice-president at the University of Tulsa. He was also a Carnegie Science Fellow at Stanford University, served as a postdoctoral fellow at the National Astronomy and Ionosphere Center in Puerto Rico and was an associate dean at Clemson University. Duncan continues to teach and conduct scientific research and is striving to increase the school's national recognition while raising the level of academic excellence.

Part III

Walking Tours

Following are lists of sites that are historically important because of what was built there, what happened there or who lived there. Included are buildings and other features that still remain, plus a few others that are merely memories. Those that no longer exist are marked with asterisks.

Most structures are private residences, commercial establishments or educational buildings that are closed to general public access. Although they may be enjoyed from the outside, grounds and interiors are not available for viewing without the owners' prior permission.

The sites are arranged here in five sections of Winter Park, each with its own tour that begins and ends at the same place. All may be walked or completed on bicycle.

Many of the sites can be viewed by car, but several portions of the routes consist of sidewalks or one-way streets (going the wrong way), which make driving inappropriate.

The instructions given below will navigate you through the neighborhoods of Winter Park merely by watching for street signs and numbers on the buildings.

Downtown Winter Park

Site	Miles	Address	Site	Miles	Address
1	0.2	433 E. New England Ave.	27	2.2	232 N. Knowles Ave.
2	0.3	160 Alexander Pl.	28	2.3	145 Lincoln Ave.
3	0.5	315 E. New England Ave.	29	2.4	102 N. Park Ave.
4	0.5	300 E. New England Ave.	30	2.4	102 S. Park Ave.
5	0.6	300 S. Interlachen Ave.	31	2.4	110–120 S. Park Ave.
6	0.6	225 S. Interlachen Ave.	32	2.4	126–130 S. Park Ave.
7	0.7	200 S. Interlachen Ave.	33	2.5	142 S. Park Ave.
8	0.7	147 S. Interlachen Ave.	34	2.5	152 S. Park Ave.
9	0.8	311 E. Morse Blvd.	35	2.5	202 S. Park Ave.
10	0.8	189 E. Morse Blvd.	36	2.5	214–218 S. Park Ave.
11	0.9	210 E. Morse Blvd.	37	2.5	216 S. Park Ave.
12	0.9	125 N. Interlachen Ave.	38	2.6	300 S. Park Ave.
13	1.0	208 N. Interlachen Ave.	39	2.6	306 S. Park Ave.
14	1.0	231 N. Interlachen Ave.	40	2.6	307 S. Park Ave.
15	1.1	420 N. Interlachen Ave.	41	2.6	311 S. Park Ave.
16	1.2	520 N. Interlachen Ave.	42	2.6	310–326 S. Park Ave.
17	1.3	617 N. Interlachen Ave.	43	2.6	329 S. Park Ave.
18	1.3	656 N. Interlachen Ave.	44	2.6	342 S. Park Ave.
19	1.4	761 Old England Ave.	45	2.6	401 S. Park Ave.
20	1.5	656 N. Park Ave.	46	2.7	400 S. Park Ave.
21	1.7	640 N. Park Ave.	47	2.7	451 S. Park Ave.
22	1.8	520–540 N. Knowles Ave.	48	2.8	143 W. Fairbanks Ave.
23	2.0	348 N. Park Ave.	49	3.1	428 S. Interlachen Ave.
24	2.0	312–316 N. Park Ave.	50	3.1	419 S. Interlachen Ave.
25	2.1	252 N. Park Ave.	51	3.2	377 E. Fairbanks Ave.
26	2.1	200–218 N. Park Ave.		3.4	End

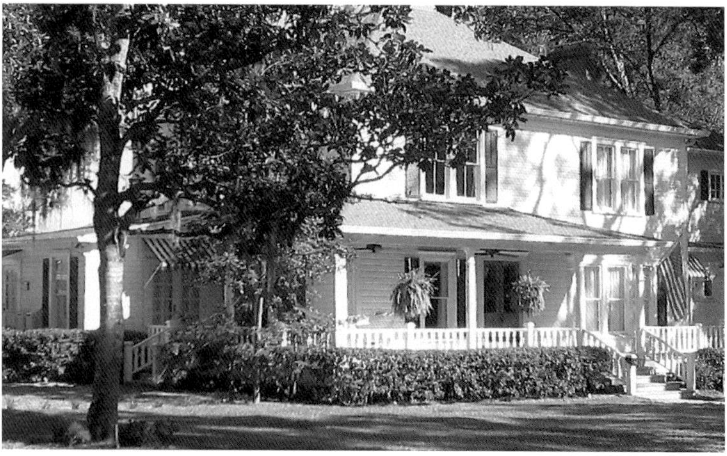

WEBSTER-WAGNER HOUSE
This house has eighty-eight windows and no two are exactly the same size. This arts and crafts–style cottage was the first recipient of the Winter Park Historical Association's Heritage Plaque to recognize its significance in the history of the city. *Photo by Gayle Prince Rajtar.*

Begin on Ollie Avenue (a block south of Fairbanks Avenue), adjacent to the park at Dinky Dock. Then go north on Ollie, cross Fairbanks at the light, head north on Chase Avenue and west on New England Avenue.

(1) 433 EAST NEW ENGLAND AVENUE

WEBSTER-WAGNER HOUSE

This home was built in 1905 by Albert Wagner and his invalid sister-in-law Jean Webster. The house was originally square with open porches on brick piers. A two-story addition in the 1930s included a paneled chapel and library installed by an Episcopal bishop named Matthews that was later used as a music room. The bishop married a member of the family that owned Procter & Gamble, manufacturers of cleaning products. The local joke was that in this home, "cleanliness was next to godliness."

Continue west on New England Avenue and head north on Alexander Place.

(2) 160 ALEXANDER PLACE

MCALLASTER HOUSE

In 1934, James Gamble Rogers II designed this Spanish eclectic–style home for Archibald and Lena McAllaster featuring a *U*-

shaped courtyard in the front as part of its entryway. Its original roof tiles were hand formed in Spain and came from the same place as those used in Casa Feliz—the Penney Farms community in North Florida, which the founder of the J.C. Penney Company had been developing before he experienced financial difficulty.

Head south on Alexander Place and continue west on New England Avenue.

(3) 315 EAST NEW ENGLAND AVENUE

*TANTUM-SCHULTZ COTTAGE

Dr. J.R. Tantum, a homeopathic doctor, moved to Winter Park in 1881 and built a home at this site in 1883. He was briefly the president of the Winter Park Hotel Company. Tantum died in 1887, and three years later the home was acquired by William Schultz Jr. Banker J.R. List acquired it in 1912 and his wife, known as Aunt Hat, operated it as an exclusive tea room. Robert E. Langford Sr. and Herbert Halverstadt purchased the home in 1945. In 1948–50, the twenty-four-unit Langford Apartments were built on the site, necessitating the moving of the cottage to 200 South Interlachen Avenue. The apartments were torn down in the mid-2000s and replaced by The Trovillion condominiums.

(4) 300 EAST NEW ENGLAND AVENUE

*LANGFORD HOTEL

In January of 1956, the 82-room Langford Hotel designed by William B. Harvard Jr. had its grand opening with a dinner dance in its fifth-floor Tree Top Room. It was the project of Robert E. Langford Sr. of Chicago, who had built apartments across the street and also wanted a year-round hotel. The Langford was the area's first hotel with air conditioning. It was expanded with a seven-story addition in 1971 made by stacking modular units manufactured in San Antonio. The hotel, which had grown to 218 rooms, celebrated its farewell banquet on May 17, 2000, and was torn down to make room for a modern hotel to be constructed later.

Head south on Interlachen Avenue.

(5) 300 SOUTH INTERLACHEN AVENUE

*PANSY COTTAGE

Dr. Gustavus Alden built a home here for his wife, Isabella Macdonald Alden, author of the "Pansy" books of the 1880s. In about 1900, banker Michael M. Smith bought the house

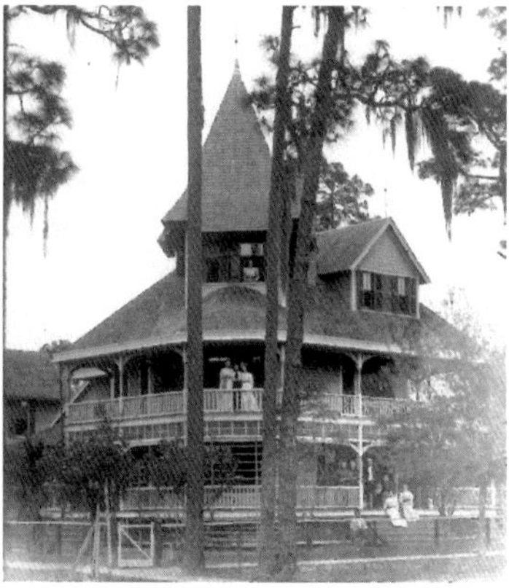

PANSY COTTAGE
This is an 1880s image of the Alden home at the corner of Interlachen and Lyman Avenues. It was acquired in 1929 by Luther Detwiler, who turned it into a rooming house. Pansy Cottage was torn down in 1955 and the site is now occupied by The Residences, a condominium complex. *Courtesy of the Florida Photographic Collection.*

when it had no electricity, no plumbing and a wood stove in the kitchen, all very typical for the era. The home was also known as the Peschman Inn.

Head north on Interlachen Avenue.

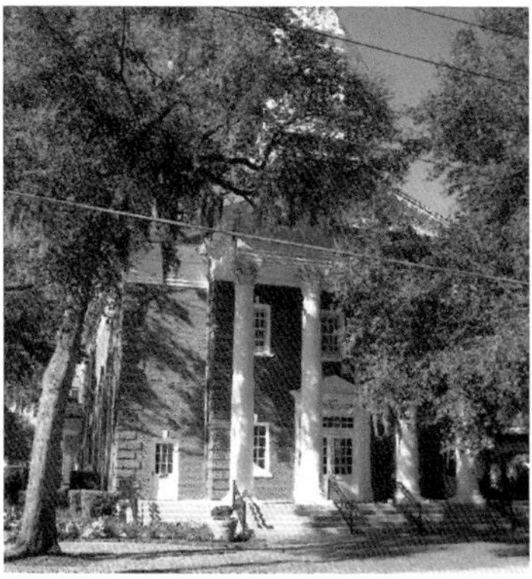

FIRST CONGREGATIONAL CHURCH
This is how the colonial-style Congregational Church appears today. On the church grounds are a fellowship hall and office built in 1940 and 1958, respectively, based on the designs of James Gamble Rogers II. James Gamble Rogers III designed the Sunday school building and arcade added in 1963. *Photo by Gayle Prince Rajtar.*

(6) 225 South Interlachen Avenue

First Congregational Church of Winter Park

The present Old Lyme colonial-style sanctuary was designed by W.H. Nicklas of Cleveland, assisted by Howard M. Reynolds of Orlando, and was completed in 1924. Grounds and parking lots were expanded from time to time by the acquisition and removal of adjacent homes. In 1937, the Winter Park Congregational Church was renamed as the Congregational-Christian Church of Winter Park and took on its present name of First Congregational Church of Winter Park in 1961.

(7) 200 South Interlachen Avenue

*Lacy Shadows

This was the site of Judge J.F. Welbourne's cottage until it was moved across the street in 1910. In 1948, the Tantum-Schultz

Cottage was moved here, its verandas were removed and it was divided into six apartments. In 1952, Mr. and Mrs. James Crum bought it, added fancy ironwork and named it Lacy Shadows. In 1977, it was sold to William A. Selley, a salesman for the Winter Park Land Company. Twenty years later, it was purchased by Denarich Construction, which tore down Lacy Shadows and replaced it with the five-story Versailles Condominiums.

(8) 147 SOUTH INTERLACHEN AVENUE

*ONEONTA LODGE

Dentist J.E. Brecht had a home built here in 1886 on six acres that stretched to Lake Osceola. The next owner, J.H. Wyeth, added electricity, a first for homes in Winter Park, and in 1889 he added an ornamental fence. In 1910, Dr. and Mrs. Jerry Allen Trovillion bought the home and renamed it Trovillion's Grove. Trovillion opened a pharmacy on Park Avenue in 1908 and had a local medical practice. The home was razed in 1989 to make room for a $4.5 million condominium development.

At Morse Boulevard, look to the east.

(9) 311 EAST MORSE BOULEVARD

*LYMAN HOUSE

Frederick Lyman built his home here in 1888 with a view of Lake Osceola. Later owners included Dr. and Mrs. William F. Blackman while he was the president of Rollins College in 1902–03. For a time, it housed the Green Gables Tea Room, then became the home of Walter and Louise Schultz. It was later known as the President's House while it was owned by the college. It was sold by the college and burned in 1959. The site is now occupied by Whispering Waters Condominiums.

Head west on Morse Boulevard.

(10) 189 EAST MORSE BOULEVARD

LINCOLN APARTMENTS

This forty-two-unit apartment house was built in 1926 during the Florida Land Boom. The land was sold in 1925 for $12,000, $18,000 and $25,000, winding up in the hands of the Lincoln Investment Company, which built the apartments. In 2001, it was acquired by the First Methodist Church, which renovated nearly every portion of it, keeping intact only the elaborate south entrance.

Head east on Morse Boulevard.

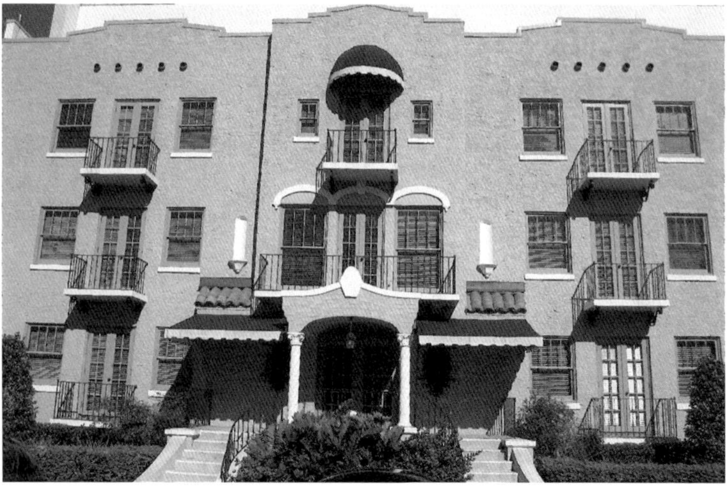

Lincoln Apartments
Today's building is very different from the one erected in 1926 as high-class living space with reasonable rental rates. Most of the Lincoln was torn down, leaving only the southern entrance to remind one of its former elegance. Inside now are church offices, classrooms and a gymnasium. *Photo by Gayle Prince Rajtar.*

(11) 210 East Morse Boulevard

El Cortez Apartments

These wood-frame residences were constructed in 1922, and have been maintained with their original appearance.

Continue east on Morse Boulevard and head north on Interlachen Avenue.

(12) 125 North Interlachen Avenue

First United Methodist Church of Winter Park

On May 7, 1967, the present sanctuary was dedicated. Stained-glass windows were created by the J.&R. Lamb Studios Inc. of Tenafly, New Jersey. Rogers, Lovelock and Fritz designed the sanctuary and the general contractor was Allen Trovillion.

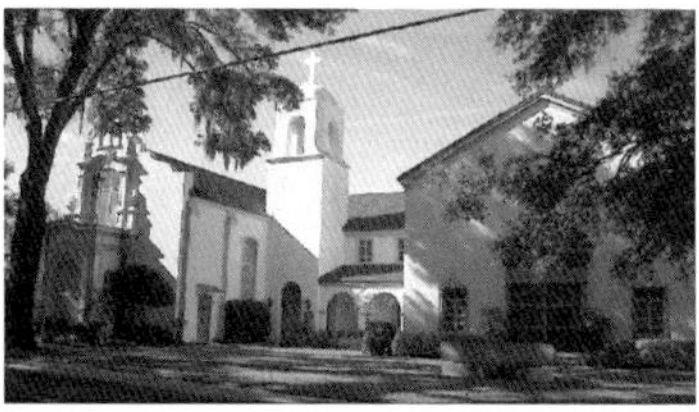

First United Methodist Church
This is the third Methodist sanctuary built on this lot. The present 1967 building replaced one made of hollow tile and stucco, trimmed with stone. It featured a fifty-six-foot tower that supported a large illuminated cross. *Photo by Gayle Prince Rajtar.*

(13) 208 North Interlachen Avenue

Holt-Mumby House

This home was built for Mrs. S.F. Pryor in 1922. Ten years later, it was acquired by Rollins College as a home for its president. Here, Hamilton Holt entertained students and visitors, granted honorary degrees and represented the college to the public. After Holt retired in 1949, it served as an off-campus residence hall, sorority house, art museum and chancellor's office. It was bought by Robert C. and Peggy W. Mumby in 1979, and they added a terrace and swimming pool.

(14) 231 North Interlachen Avenue

Osceola Lodge

Francis Knowles built this home in 1882 as a winter resort to attract visitors, and he and his family wintered in it for a few years before his death. It was originally surrounded by orange trees and a white picket fence. In 1945, Hugh McKean and Jeannette Genius married and moved into the home.

(15) 420 North Interlachen Avenue

*Chapman Cottage

In 1882, Oliver Chapman built a home here resembling a rustic lodge. It was Winter Park's first permanent residence and had a large, sloping shingle roof and a porch on the south and eastern sides facing the lake. It was torn down in 1938 and was replaced by a new home for the McKinney family. The twenty-room house is now known as the Haskell Estate.

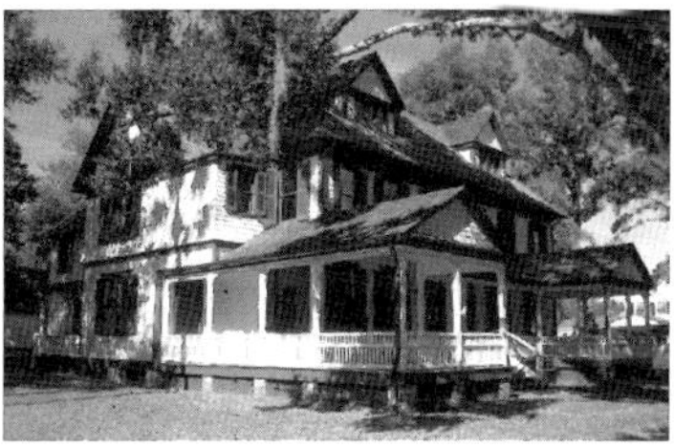

Osceola Lodge
When Charles Morse bought this home in 1904, he named it Osceola Lodge and renovated it with a craftsman style using native building materials, emphasizing functionalism, ease of maintenance and comfort. He also doubled its size. *Photo by Gayle Prince Rajtar.*

(16) 520 North Interlachen Avenue

Capen House

James S. Capen visited the area in 1884 and soon returned to live there permanently. The first portion of this home was built in 1885 at a cost of about $825. Extensive additions included bathrooms and a stucco interior. The original open front porch was converted into an enclosed reception room. It is easily identified by its half-timbered gables. Capen raised grapefruit and was an organizer of the Orlando–Winter Park Railroad Company and the secretary of the Winter Park Land Company.

(17) 617 NORTH INTERLACHEN AVENUE

VILLA HERMOSA

This Spanish eclectic–style home was designed in 1934 by James Gamble Rogers II for painter George L. Noyes and his wife Mabel. Included in its twenty-five hundred square feet was one bedroom, an art studio, an office and a side courtyard. The home has an entrance on the south end of the property, but its major focus is away from streets, toward a courtyard defined by a *U*-shaped wall. There is a full-sized basement beneath its kitchen. George and Mabel moved to Vermont and the home was purchased by Tracy Lay, who had Rogers design an addition in 1939.

(18) 656 NORTH INTERLACHEN AVENUE

*ERGOOD-ROE-TOUSEY COTTAGE

Previously on this site, before the construction of Casa Feliz, was the Ergood-Roe-Tousey Cottage, built in 1887 for John R. Ergood, the city's first postmaster. He arrived in 1881 and the mild climate cured his lung hemorrhages. The home's tall, square tower topped by a domed cupola provided a magnificent view of Lake Osceola and the surrounding countryside. Later owners included Colonel John H. Roe (who called the house "Bellwood") and Charles G. Tousey.

Head north on Old England Avenue.

(19) 761 OLD ENGLAND AVENUE

WINTER PARK COUNTRY CLUB AND CHARLES H. MORSE MEMORIAL PARK

Charles Morse helped organize the country club in 1914, the year the clubhouse was built, and leased land to it for a dollar per year. The club went inactive in 1925, but in 1937 it was reactivated. Arthur Harris obtained permission for dual use by the country club and the University Club, and that continued from 1937 until 1948, when the University Club moved to a new building.

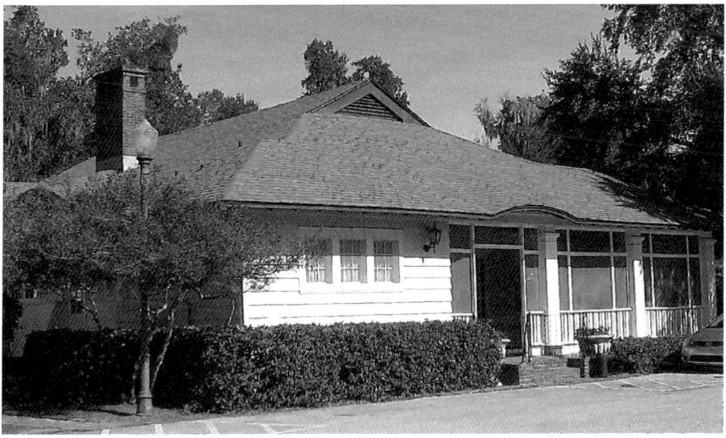

COUNTRY CLUB

The golf course once stretched from here to the later site of the Winter Park Mall, making it the second-largest course in the South. The country club and course have been city owned since 1997, and two years later they were added to the National Register of Historic Places. *Photo by Gayle Prince Rajtar.*

Walk west through the Country Club parking lot to the large stone house.

(20) 656 NORTH PARK AVENUE

CASA FELIZ

This 5,400-square-foot home was originally located at 656 North Interlachen Avenue. Named "Casa Feliz" (Happy House), it was built in 1932 at a cost of $28,000 for Robert

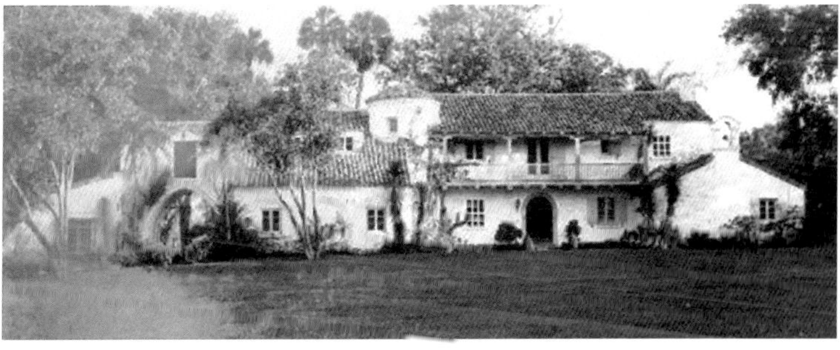

CASA FELIZ

In 2000, the new owners of the former Barbour residence announced their desire to demolish it and replace it with a home with larger rooms. The following year, $1.2 million was raised to move the home three hundred yards across the street to its present site adjacent to the golf course. *Courtesy of the Florida Photographic Collection.*

B. Barbour. Designed by James Gamble Rogers II, it resembles an old Andalusian cortijo, a family courtyard farmhouse. Even when new, it looked old because of the use of older materials, including bricks from the demolished Orlando Armory. Roof tiles came from Barcelona, where peasants formed them on their thighs to give them proper curvature. The roof was designed with a six-inch sag to simulate age.

Walk through the arch at the north end of the house, then continue west on the sidewalk and south on Park Avenue.

(21) 640 North Park Avenue

The Park-Aire

This apartment complex was built in 1956 with an attractive interior courtyard. It was converted to condominiums in 1988 and retains its art moderne character.

Continue south on Park Avenue, head east on Swoope Avenue and south on Knowles Avenue.

(22) 520–540 North Knowles Avenue

Barbour Apartments

These apartments, also known as The Abbey, were designed in 1933 for Robert Barbour by James Gamble Rogers II. It is a string of seven attached sections of differing shapes and sizes that avoids a typical rectangular apartment appearance. The several chimney pots also add an interesting touch.

Continue south on Knowles Avenue, head west on Canton Avenue and south on Park Avenue.

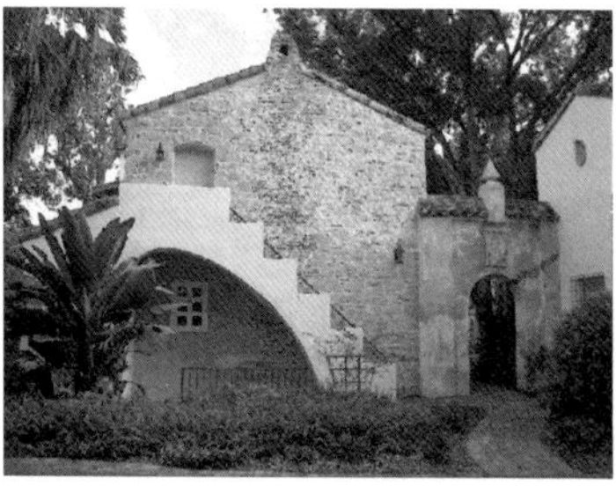

Barbour Apartments
This apartment complex featuring differing shapes, sizes and arrangements of units is best known for the exterior stairway shown in this photo. Its unusual asymmetrical arch combines an interesting appearance with functionality. *Photo by Steve Rajtar.*

(23) 348 North Park Avenue

Little Europe Block Garden Shops

In 1948, Eve Proctor Morrill moved to Winter Park. Here, she founded the Proctor Shops, which offered the latest fashions.

During the 1950s, she advocated the placement of brick planters and the remodeling of the Park Avenue shops to look like those found in European villages. During the 1960s, her urging resulted in the establishment of Hidden Gardens and the garden shops at this location.

(24) 312–316 North Park Avenue

Wren Taylor Building

This building was erected in 1925–26, housing two stores downstairs and four apartments upstairs. It is occupied today by dentists, an art store and a jeweler.

(25) 252 North Park Avenue

Winter Park Sun Building

In June 1953, Eve M. Bacon established the *Winter Park Sun* newspaper, which was published in this building. It came out every Thursday until April 1, 1959, when it became part of the *Winter Park Sun-Herald*. This building was also the home of the Yum Yum Shoppe, where customers could make their own ice cream sundaes.

(26) 200–218 North Park Avenue

Jacobson's

This retail building was constructed in 1956 and for many years has housed the Jacobson's clothing store.

Continue south on Park Avenue, head east on Lincoln Avenue and north on Knowles Avenue.

(27) 232 North Knowles Avenue

Knowles Cottage 1

Francis Knowles built this home and two others in 1886–87 for resale to prospective customers. The construction price of this one with heart pine siding was about $3,500. Knowles was a major stockholder of the Winter Park Company, and for a time this was used as his office. It was also once owned by Charles Morse, who used it for guests who visited his family at Osceola Lodge.

Head south on Knowles Avenue to Lincoln Avenue.

(28) 145 LINCOLN AVENUE

KNOWLES COTTAGE 2

This cottage was built in 1886–87 by Francis Knowles for resale. During the 1980s, it was substantially renovated for use as the office of the architectural firm of Rogers, Lovelock and Fritz.

Head west on Lincoln Avenue and south on Park Avenue.

(29) 102 NORTH PARK AVENUE

ERGOOD BUILDING

When built by Loring Chase in 1882, this structure (also known as the Ramsey Building) was called the Pioneer Store, which sold groceries, clothing, furniture, hay, grain and numerous other items. It was the first structure on Park Avenue and was made of wood. The upstairs hall was used for social functions and doubled as the first school, church, town hall and post office. The lower floor was leased to John R. Ergood and Robert White Jr. for a store. The Pioneer Store business, which was sold to A.H. Paul in 1888, Andrew MacCallum in 1897 and William Schultz Jr., was moved south one block to another building by 1900. In 1914, this structure was covered with a brick veneer and the front porches were removed. It housed a pharmacy for many years, beginning with Maxson's Drug Store in 1900, followed by the Trovillion Drug Store operated by Dr. Jerry A. Trovillion from 1908 to 1914. Later uses have included professional offices and retail shops.

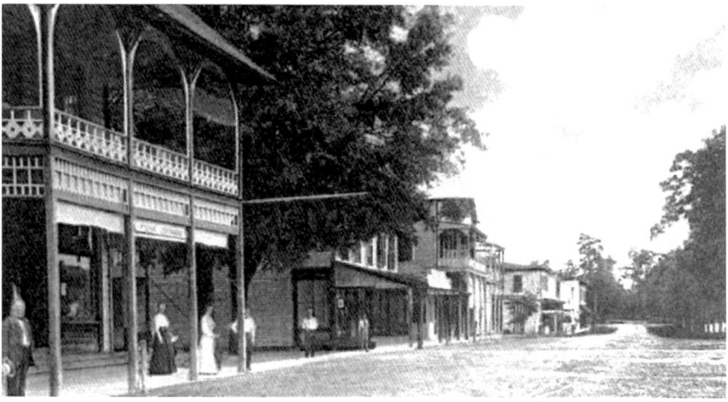

ERGOOD BUILDING

This is one of the oldest remaining structures, and also one of the most modified. In this photo, the Ergood Building is all the way to the left and shows the addition of a two-story porch with a broad roof. Compare this to the next photo, which shows the building in 1888 with Ergood's name still visible atop the one-story porch roof. *Courtesy of the Florida Photographic Collection.*

(30) 102 SOUTH PARK AVENUE

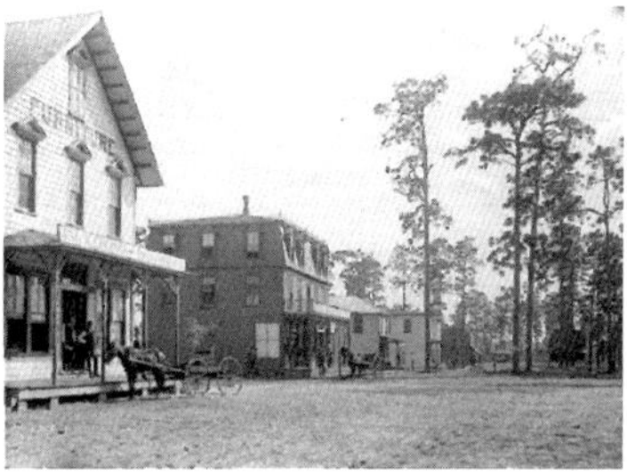

PARKWOOD BUILDING
The second building from the left was built in 1883 by Mr. Hill, then was bought by Jonathan Symonds and Loring Chase in 1884. Charles J. Ladd acquired it in 1886 and opened Ladd's Hardware & Drugs in it. He sold it in 1901 to Forney Shepherd for his general store. *Courtesy of the Florida Photographic Collection.*

PARKWOOD BUILDING

This was Winter Park's first brick commercial structure. Forney Shepherd built it in 1912 to replace his 1883 wooden building, and he called the new one the F.W. Shepherd Building. Its first occupant was Bumby Hardware, a branch of the large Orlando store. In 1923, Shepherd sold the building to W.H. Hale, who opened a grocery store in it. Later tenants included Watkins Paint and Wallpaper beginning in 1955, Columbia Jewelers and Park Avenue Eyewear.

(31) 110–120 SOUTH PARK AVENUE

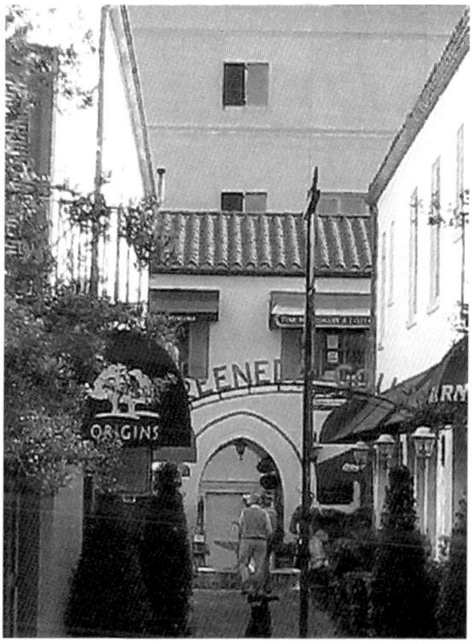

GREENEDA COURT
The original pair of two-story masonry structures had shops downstairs and small apartments upstairs. In 1946, another mixed-use building was added at the back of the lot, creating a peaceful, sheltered courtyard just feet from busy Park Avenue traffic. *Photo by Gayle Prince Rajtar.*

GREENEDA COURT

This group of retail buildings with a courtyard was designed by James Gamble Rogers II in 1945 for Ray Greene, a realtor and former Winter Park mayor. Previously, the site included the headquarters of the Safety Cab Company, established by J.T. Ellis in 1932.

(32) 126–130 SOUTH PARK AVENUE

MORSE BLOCK

In 1885, the Winter Park Company was formed with a capitalization of $300,000 to develop and promote Winter Park. Its initial officers

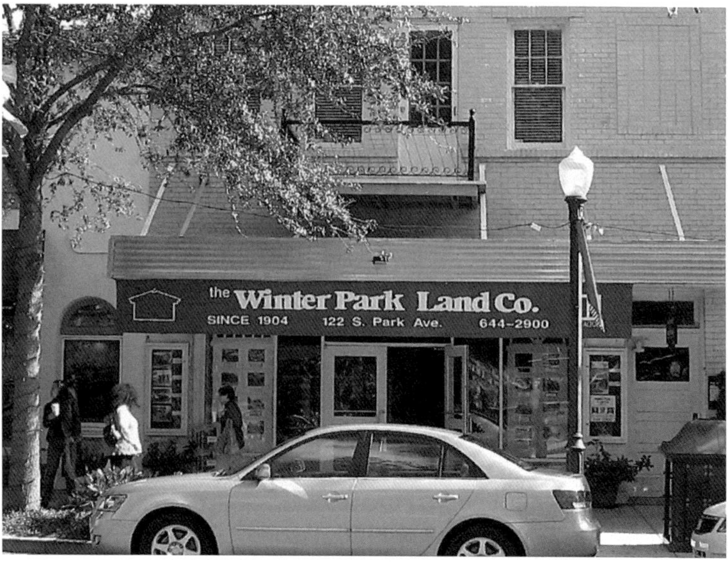

WINTER PARK LAND COMPANY
This building's tenants included the Baby Grande Theatre owned by Braxton Beacham, who took the name from the Grande Theatre he owned in Orlando. The 1917 theater was rebuilt in 1927 and a $10,000 pipe organ was installed. The Baby Grande closed in 1940, reopened in 1947 and later closed permanently. *Photo by Gayle Prince Rajtar.*

and directors were Frederick Lyman of Minnesota, Franklin Fairbanks of Vermont, F.G. Webster of Massachusetts, Loring Chase, Alonzo Rollins, William Comstock of Chicago and Judge J.F. Welbourne. In 1904, Charles Morse founded the Winter Park Land Company, which bought twelve hundred town lots, orange groves and wild land from the Winter Park Company. That gave Morse's company ownership of nearly half of the town. For $15,000 in 1917, he built this Morse Block as the city's first modern offices for his company, which shared the building with the offices of Harold Ward and Herbert Barnum, the WCTU Reading Room and the Baby Grande Theatre.

(33) 142 SOUTH PARK AVENUE

POST OFFICE AND BANK

In 1911, the building now housing the Williams-Sonoma store was built for the post office and the first Bank of Winter Park with a shuttered portion in between, set back a few feet from the sidewalk. That year, the bank's officers were President William Blackman, Vice-President Harold Ward and Cashier C.D. Powell.

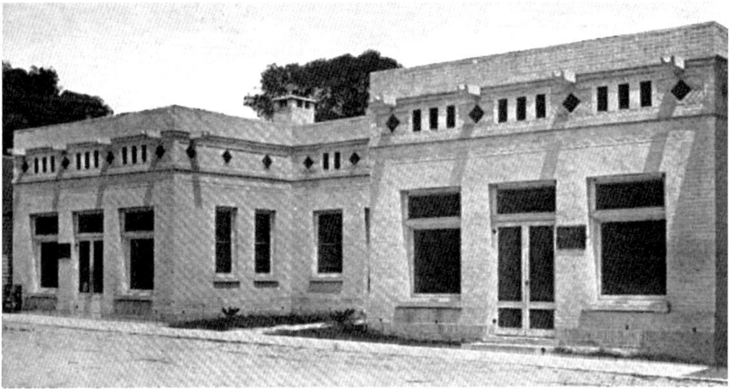

BANK OF WINTER PARK
When the bank ceased to occupy the southern portion of this complex (on the right in this photo), a secure vault remained. One of the later retail occupants, the Golden Cricket gallery, utilized the vault for Christmas displays. *Courtesy of the Florida Photographic Collection.*

(34) 152 SOUTH PARK AVENUE

PIONEER BUILDING

The first mayor, Robert White Jr., built White's Hall here, housing his general store in 1884 after splitting from John Ergood the year before. William Schultz Jr. moved the Pioneer Store into this building by 1900, and it was inherited by his sons Arthur, Lee and Walter in 1907. In 1921, it was sold to Girard Denning, who had arrived in 1894 and in 1909 became the youngest mayor of the city at age twenty-three. During 1929, Denning moved the Pioneer Store to 230 South Park Avenue and continued to sell general merchandise there until 1935. That year, Roy Hough, the owner of the Sanitary Market located next door, purchased Denning's business and combined the two to make Hough's Food Store, which continued until the middle of the next decade.

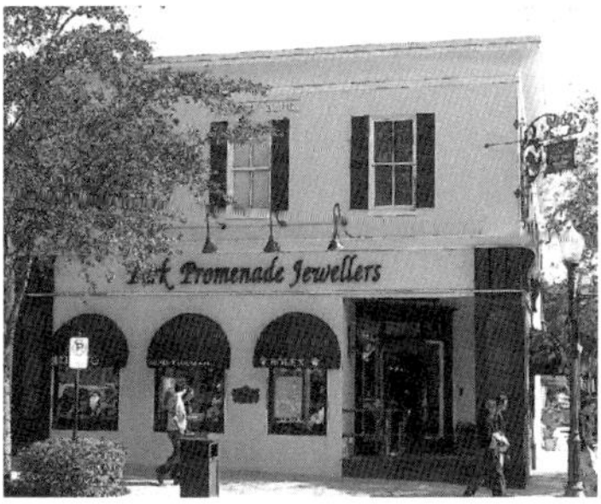

PIONEER BUILDING
This building started out as a white wooden structure with a tin roof. Over the years, it has been substantially modified, including the application of a brick overlay during the mid-1920s. It was again remodeled in 1956 to bring it closer to today's appearance. *Photo by Gayle Prince Rajtar.*

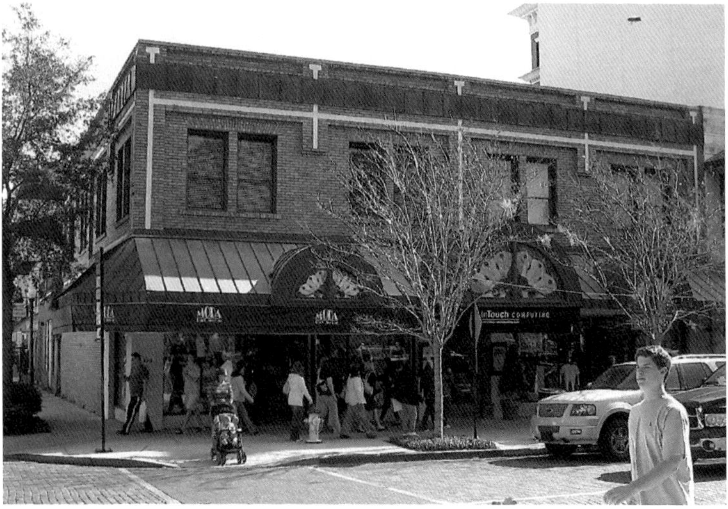

SCHULTZ BUILDING
A bicycle shop on this corner was eliminated to make room for this 1916 structure, built for Walter Schultz to house his Men's Store. Later, it was enlarged by the addition of a one-story extension in the rear. *Photo by Gayle Prince Rajtar.*

(35) 202 SOUTH PARK AVENUE

SHULTZ BUILDING

During the 1920s, this was Miss Vicks' Hat Shop, operated by Mrs. J.C. Vicks. She sold it to Robert F. Leedy, who arrived in 1919 and partnered with Roland Hotard in a drugstore at another address. Shortly thereafter, Leedy moved his business to another building and sold this one to R.C. Baker for his clothing store. In 1956, Baker sold the business and building to Mr. and Mrs. Paul Wrenn, who ran Wrenn's Men's Furnishings until it closed in the early 1980s.

(36) 214–218 SOUTH PARK AVENUE

*HENKEL BLOCK

The buildings that originally stood here were collectively known as the Henkel Block, built by Dr. Miller A. Henkel. He came from Virginia in 1883 in search of a climate that would give his wife relief from her tuberculosis, and for many years he was the town's only practicing physician. James Capen had a real estate office here (Capen & Company) beginning in 1886, and other tenants included Dr. J.L.B. Eager's Seminole Pharmacy, Maxson's Bookstore, Pierce and Matthews Market and Dr. Henkel's office. A shed-roofed porch supported by simple posts

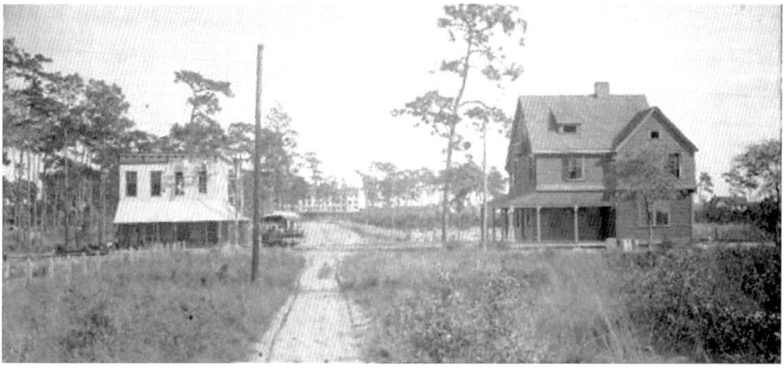

VIEW DOWN NEW ENGLAND AVENUE
This is a mid-1880s view eastward toward Park Avenue. On the left is the beginning of the Henkel Block and on the right is the Winter Park Company office. Between the two, the Seminole Hotel appears in the distance. *Courtesy of the Florida Photographic Collection.*

provided the city's only shaded sidewalk. In 1952, a new bank building replaced the Henkel Block, and five years later it became the home of the First National Bank of Winter Park, later a part of Barnett Bank and then Bank of America.

(37) 216 SOUTH PARK AVENUE

PANNULLO'S ITALIAN RESTAURANT

This building opened as the Rexall Drug Store in 1937 and that business continued until 1981, with Happy Jack's Sandwich Shack located in the back in 1972–81. Bombay's was located here in 1981–82, followed by Good Earth (1983–85), the Fishery (1985–87) and Sbarro's (1987–93). Pannullo's Italian Restaurant was founded in 1993 and remains a popular eatery.

(38) 300 SOUTH PARK AVENUE

UNION STATE BANK BUILDING

In 1917, this brick structure was built for the Union State Bank founded that year by Edward F Keezel, one of only two local banks that remained open during the Great Depression. In 1930, when the government declared a bank holiday, closing them to prevent a run on the cash they had on reserve, A. Irving Bacheller and George Kraft personally guaranteed this bank's securities and convinced regulators to allow it to remain open. It is now the home of the Peterbrooke Chocolatier.

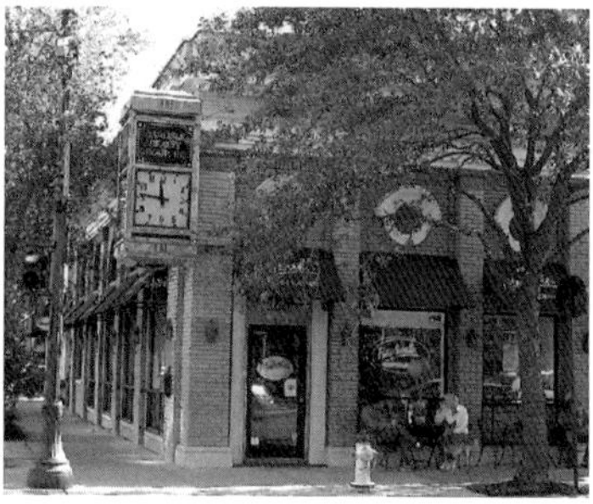

UNION STATE BANK
This building's original use as a bank is shown by its stately columns, representing strength and security. Over the years, however, it has also been the home of other businesses, including Orange Hardware & Furniture, which E.R. Baldwin acquired in 1927 and renamed the Baldwin Hardware Store. *Photo by Gayle Prince Rajtar.*

(39) 306 SOUTH PARK AVENUE

TAYLOR'S PHARMACY

This business was founded by W.J. Taylor in the Ramsey Building and opened in October 1948. The drugstore operated there until 1987, when it moved to 230 North Park Avenue. In 1999 it relocated to this site, where it remains.

(40) 307 SOUTH PARK AVENUE

PARK PLAZA HOTEL

The earlier wooden building erected on this site in 1886 was the home of the Winter Park Company. Built in 1922 by M.J. Kramer, the present brick structure was known as the Hamilton Hotel until 1977, when it was bought by Cissie and John Spang.

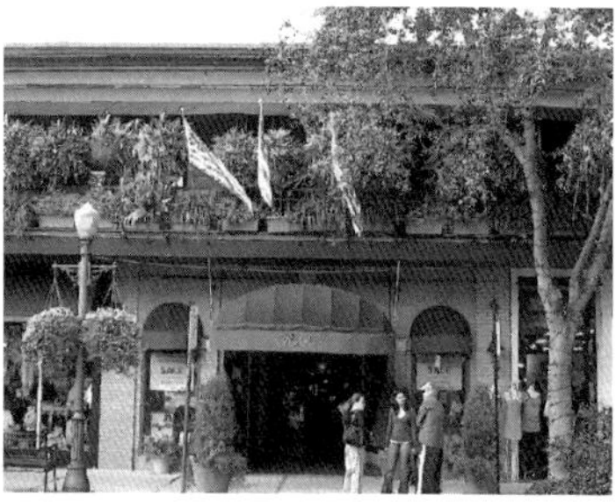

PARK PLAZA HOTEL
The hotel lobby downstairs retains its 1920s charm and elegance, and guests are led upstairs to their rooms that access the 1932 balcony overlooking Park Avenue. Commercial tenants downstairs included the A&P Grocery Store, which opened in 1923. *Photo by Gayle Prince Rajtar.*

(41) 311 SOUTH PARK AVENUE

LEEDY'S

In about 1930, Robert F. Leedy moved his small department store here from across the street. His daughter, Lorraine Leedy Stewart, took over management in 1949 and became the store's owner in 1954. Reba Campbell became the owner in 1962, and she operated it until August 1985. The space is now occupied by Bébé's children's store.

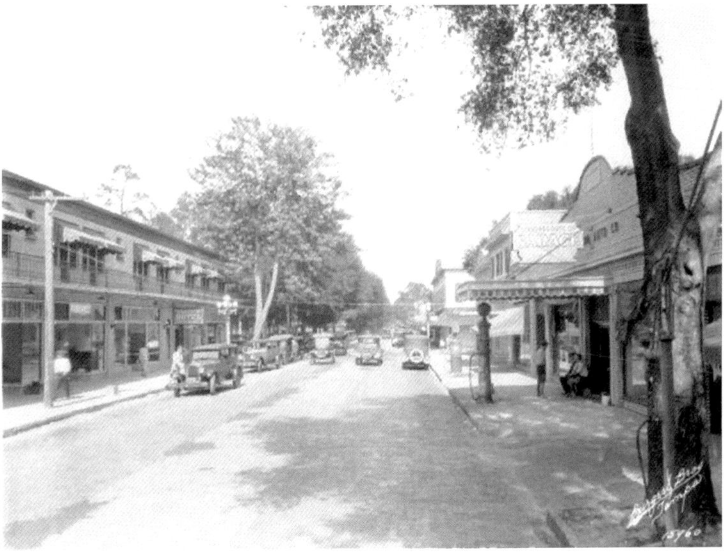

KEEZEL BLOCK
Park Avenue has changed since this 1925 photo, but many buildings from that period remain. On the left is the Hamilton Hotel before the addition of its wrought-iron balcony. On the right of the gas pump is the Standard Auto garage, whose tenants now include the Nicole Miller clothing store. *Courtesy of the Florida Photographic Collection.*

(42) 310–326 SOUTH PARK AVENUE

KEEZEL BLOCK

In 1916, this was the location of the Standard Auto garage. In 1921, Edward Keezel built an adjacent brick structure, which housed the Orange Hardware and Furniture Company. Two years later, the Martin Brothers Five-, Ten- and Twenty-five-cent Store opened here. Keezel added more stores running to the intersection with Lyman Avenue in 1924.

(43) 329 SOUTH PARK AVENUE

COLONY THEATER

This art deco–style theater opened in 1940. For most of its existence as a theater, the Colony was open to white individuals only. Black moviegoers had available to them the Star Theatre (also known as the Famous Theatre), located at 260 West New England Avenue. Competition from multi-screen theater complexes caused the Colony to close in 1975, and it was converted into restaurants and shops.

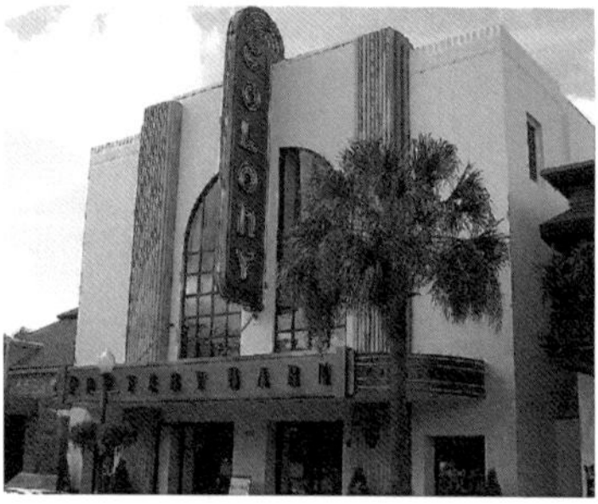

Colony Theater
After the theater closed in 1975, it was transformed into an arcade that included a Barnie's Coffee and Tea Company shop. The façade was kept when, in 1996, the building was remodeled into a Pottery Barn store. *Photo by Gayle Prince Rajtar.*

(44) 342 South Park Avenue

C See

In 1949, Al Beasley opened the Toggery in this building, specializing in conservative preppy clothes for students, plus career clothing for professional men. The store was sold in 1975 to John Dixon, who in 1990 shifted its focus from clothing to gifts and tourist items. By 1992, Park Books occupied the space, later followed by C See, an eyeglass boutique.

(45) 401 South Park Avenue

City Hall

The first town hall was located above Ergood's General Store in the Ergood Building. The present city hall was built in 1962–64.

(46) 400 South Park Avenue

*Park Avenue School (Winter Park Graded School)

When built in 1914–16, the first half of the school cost $30,000. Its first classes had 150 pupils in eleven grades that were taught by ten teachers. The second half was completed in 1922. In 1927, grades seven through twelve were moved to a new school on Huntington Avenue, and for many years this remained an elementary school. It was purchased in 1961 by Rollins College and was used for regular classes, professors' offices and its School for Continuing Education. The structure was razed in 1989 and the site was turned into a parking lot. It was redeveloped in 1997–99 into the Rollins Parking Garage and the SunTrust Plaza retail shops including the Gap, Restoration Hardware and Merrill Lynch.

(47) 451 SOUTH PARK AVENUE

*SHUFFLEBOARD CLUB

This was the location of the Winter Park Shuffleboard Club, which competed with clubs from other Central Florida communities. By 1955, the Winter Park club had more than 450 members, and it moved to another location during the mid-1960s.

Continue south on Park Avenue and walk west on Fairbanks Avenue.

(48) 143 WEST FAIRBANKS AVENUE

MILLER'S HARDWARE

In 1940, Robert R. Miller opened a Ben Franklin Store on Park Avenue. He sold it in 1944, bought the present building and founded Miller's Hardware in 1945. After he died in 1962, the business was acquired by partners Bob A. Miller and Cliff Canada. Later operated by Steve Miller, it is Winter Park's oldest continuously operated family business.

Head east on Fairbanks Avenue and north on Interlachen Avenue.

(49) 428 SOUTH INTERLACHEN AVENUE

WILLIAM E. WINDERWEEDLE MEMORIAL CENTER

The Winter Park Library was built here in 1901–02 at a cost of $200, plus $25 for furnishings. Wings were added on the north and south sides in 1925, and the Mary Wattles Garden was enclosed in 1956–57 to create a meeting room. In 1979, All Saints Episcopal Church bought the building and named it after its senior warden who had died earlier that year. It was extensively remodeled in 1980 with funds from the Edyth Bush Charitable Foundation and church members. The center, including its Kingsley Auditorium, was dedicated in 1981.

(50) 419 SOUTH INTERLACHEN AVENUE

WOMAN'S CLUB

The classical revival–style clubhouse of the Woman's Club of Winter Park was designed by L. Percival Hutton and was built by L.C. Townsend in 1920. It hosted its first club meeting on January 21, 1921. The building was added to the National Register of Historic Places in 1995.

Head south on Interlachen Avenue and west on Fairbanks Avenue.

(51) 377 EAST FAIRBANKS AVENUE

THE FORTNIGHTLY INN

This 1922 house was built for Dr. Charles E. Coffin, who became president of the Fortnightly Club, a group involved in the early social and intellectual development of Winter Park. Members told stories and read poetry at their meetings held here, often followed by a dessert of cake and ice cream served by high school girls. The building now is the Glennon House, part of the All Saints Episcopal Church.

Walk northeast on Fairbanks Avenue and south on Ollie Avenue to return to the beginning of the tour.

Hannibal Square

Site	Miles	Address	Site	Miles	Address
1	0.3	822 Symonds Ave.	9	1.3	425 W. Welbourne Ave.
2	0.4	274 N. Capen Ave.	10	1.4	425½ W. New England Ave.
3	0.8	733 W. Lyman Ave.	11	1.5	535 W. New England Ave.
4	0.9	753 W. Comstock Ave.	12	1.6	160 S. Pennsylvania Ave.
5	1.1	421 S. Pennsylvania Ave.	13	1.6	141 S. Pennsylvania Ave.
6	1.1	325 Hannibal Square E.	14	1.6	550 W. Morse Blvd.
7	1.2	201 Hannibal Square E.	15	1.8	721 W. New England Ave.
8	1.3	450 W. Welbourne Ave.		1.8	End

Park at Shady Park along New England Avenue, west of Pennsylvania Avenue. Go west on New England Avenue and north on Capen Avenue to Symonds Avenue.

(1) 822 Symonds Avenue

United Church of God by Faith

Established in 1948, this congregation had a sanctuary that it rebuilt at this location in 1979. At the time, the pastor was Herbert Green Jr. and the bishop was Willie W. Matthews. C.M. Fogle served as the district superintendent.

Walk north on Capen Avenue.

(2) 274 North Capen Avenue

New Hope Missionary Baptist Church

A church was erected here in 1935 under the supervision of pastor E.J. Sheffield and was rebuilt in 1953 while C.L. Jones was the pastor. It became renowned for several murals painted by André Smith, the founder of the art colony now known as the Maitland Art Center. The murals included a triptych of a black Jesus with two worshippers, Jesus cradling a reclining black man and a black family in their yard with Jesus in the background. Several members of the congregation disliked the murals, so they were taken down and burned.

Head south on Capen Avenue to Lyman Avenue.

(3) 733 West Lyman Avenue

Flowers Temple Church of God in Christ

This church was organized in 1923 and was moved into its present building in 1935 while Reverend E. Butts was the pastor.

Continue south on Capen Avenue and head west on Comstock Avenue.

(4) 753 West Comstock Avenue

Warner Chapel Primitive Baptist Church

This church was organized in 1928, and a wooden sanctuary was erected in 1934 under the supervision of Reverend J.W. Warner. Later, it moved into its present modern church at this location.

Head east on Comstock Avenue and north on Pennsylvania Avenue.

(5) 421 South Pennsylvania Avenue

Mt. Moriah Missionary Baptist Church

This church began in 1886 in the home of Reverend Charles Ambrose and his wife Missouri, and the first sanctuary was constructed in 1888. The first pastor was Reverend C.J. Smith, who served until 1911. The present sanctuary was built in 1935 at a cost of $8,500. Mt. Moriah is the oldest predominantly black church in Winter Park and has a congregation that numbers about four hundred.

Continue north on Pennsylvania Avenue and head east on Lyman Avenue.

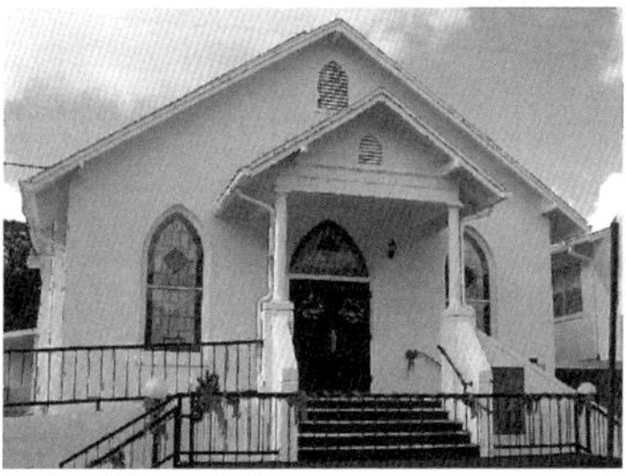

MT. MORIAH MISSIONARY BAPTIST CHURCH
Shown here is the sanctuary, built for $500 in 1892 on land donated by the Winter Park Company. Adjacent to it are a church annex and parsonage, each completed in 1959. *Photo by Steve Rajtar.*

(6) 325 HANNIBAL SQUARE EAST (AND 463 WEST LYMAN AVENUE)

*SPORTZ INN

A restaurant was opened here in 1926 by Minnie Lee and Inez Jordan with the name of Baby's Lunch Box, named after their daughter, Lessie Mae, who was nicknamed Baby Young. In 1959, Lessie Mae Marsh took over the business and renamed it the Duck Inn. In 1995, it was renamed Sportz Inn, which, for a time, was owned by Robert Knight. The building was torn down in 2006 to make room for a more modern one.

Walk north on Hannibal Square East.

(7) 201 HANNIBAL SQUARE EAST

MASONIC LODGE

Lake Hall Lodge No. 33 was founded here by the black Freemasons on January 7, 1884, and met upstairs in a two-story wooden structure. The present building, constructed by S.R. Bailey and dedicated in 1959, later was shared with the Hannibal Laundry and then a curio shop. It is still the home of Lake Hall Lodge and other fraternal organizations.

Continue north on Hannibal Square East and head east on Welbourne Avenue.

(8) 150 WEST WELBOURNE AVENUE

WELBOURNE AVENUE NURSERY AND KINDERGARTEN

This child-care facility was founded in 1929 with the original name of the Winter Park Day Nursery Association of Colored Children Incorporated.

Continue east on Welbourne Avenue.

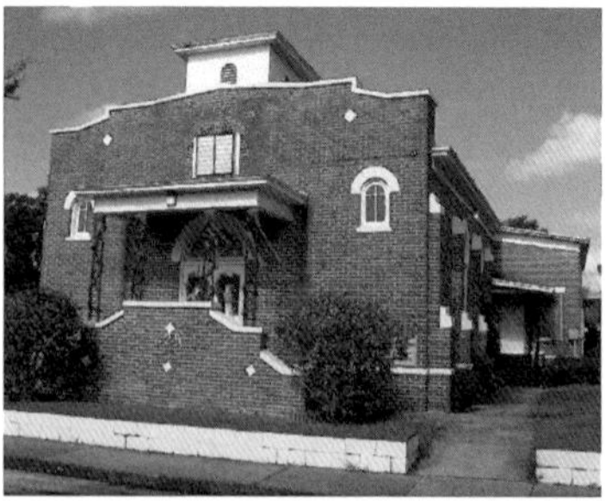

BETHEL MISSIONARY BAPTIST CHURCH
This church, called Bethel Baptist Church when it was founded in 1911, was renamed as Bethel Progressive Baptist Church, then in 1989 it incorporated with the name of Bethel Missionary Baptist Church of Winter Park. *Photo by Steve Rajtar.*

(9) 425 West Welbourne Avenue

Bethel Missionary Baptist Church

This church was formed in 1911 under the leadership of Reverend C.J. Smith, mostly by former members of Mt. Moriah Baptist Church. In 1919, Reverend E.W. Lewter became the pastor, and he was succeeded by Reverend M.L. Cherry in 1934. While he was in charge, the sanctuary was enlarged and remodeled. A lot to the east was acquired and on it was built a parsonage.

Continue east on Welbourne Avenue and head south on Virginia Avenue and west on New England Avenue.

(10) 425½ West New England Avenue

*Deluxe Barbershop

In about 1900, a barbershop was opened on the north side of the street by James Dixon Jr. and Bill Hardy, and for much of its existence, it was known as Dick & Trick's Barber Shop. It remained in operation there until 1995, when partners Alonzo Roberts and James Chandler moved it across the street. The business then known as the Deluxe Barbershop closed down permanently in early 2007.

Continue west on New England Avenue.

(11) 535 West New England Avenue

Sands Hotel

This is the oldest remaining commercial building in Hannibal Square, previously serving as a hotel in the 1940s. It furnished temporary lodging for seasonal workers and now is the Ballard & Corum Bakery shop.

Continue west on New England Avenue and head north on Pennsylvania Avenue.

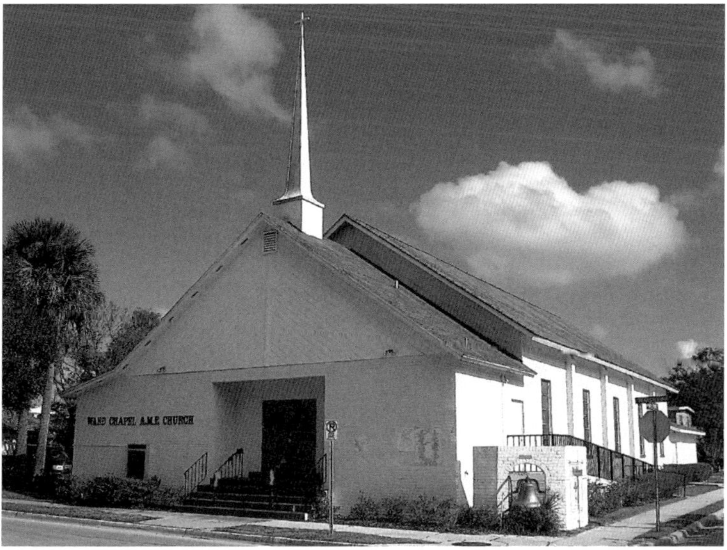

WARD CHAPEL AME CHURCH
This congregation's 1893 building was demolished in 1930 and some original building material was incorporated into the present structure, which was designed and built under the leadership of Reverend J.E. Fobb. *Photo by Steve Rajtar.*

(12) 160 SOUTH PENNSYLVANIA AVENUE

WARD CHAPEL AME CHURCH

This church began in 1893 with Reverend S.A. Williams as pastor. At the same time, a wooden church was erected on Pennsylvania Avenue, across from the present building. On February 11, 1890, while Knowles Public School served white children, a school for black children opened across Pennsylvania Avenue from the sanctuary. Later, the church auditorium was used for school functions and community gatherings.

Continue north on Pennsylvania Avenue.

(13) 141 SOUTH PENNSYLVANIA AVENUE

IDEAL WOMAN'S CLUB

The Congregational Church built the Hooker Memorial Home in 1907 to the rear of the main church building on Interlachen Avenue. In 1940, a new Hooker Memorial was erected on that site after the old home was purchased by a group of black women and moved to 120 South Pennsylvania Avenue to be the clubhouse of the Ideal Woman's Club. That home burned down in the 1990s and the club moved to this new building.

Continue north on Pennsylvania Avenue to Morse Boulevard.

(14) 550 WEST MORSE BOULEVARD

DEPUGH NURSING HOME

This nursing home, founded by Channie Laughlin of the Benevolent Club, opened in 1961. It replaced the first west side funeral home, operated by Mr. and Mrs. Richmond J. Lawson. The funeral home was moved farther north on Pennsylvania Avenue to a combination residence/business building.

Head south on Pennsylvania Avenue and west on Welbourne Court to the basketball court.

(15) 721 WEST NEW ENGLAND AVENUE

WESTSIDE LIBRARY BUILDING

The concrete block building just south of the basketball court is the original 1937 library built for black residents. It is now part of the Winter Park Community Center and is used as the headquarters of the Head Start program.

Walk south through Shady Park to the beginning of the tour.

Eastern Winter Park

Site	Miles	Address	Site	Miles	Address
1	0.1	500 Osceola Ave.	8	2.1	711 Bonita Dr.
2	0.1	550 Osceola Ave.	9	2.6	1331 Aloma Ave.
3	0.6	930 Genius Dr.	10	3.0	425 Alberta Dr.
4	0.6	1000 Genius Dr.	11	3.3	234 Detmar Dr.
5	1.2	1401 Grove Terr.	12	3.4	138 Detmar Dr.
6	1.4	1554 Harris Cir.	13	3.4	240 Trismen Terr.
7	2.1	724 Bonita Dr.	14	3.8	621 Osceola Ave.
				4.0	End

Begin on Ollie Avenue (a block south of Fairbanks Avenue), adjacent to the park at Dinky Dock. Walk north on Ollie Avenue and east on Osceola Avenue.

(1) 500 Osceola Avenue

*Batchelor Cottage

Citrus grower Richard N. Batchelor built a large home here in 1885 costing $7,000. For a time, he ran it as the Batchelor Hotel. He is credited with starting the town's beautification program by planting shade trees along its streets. The house was briefly leased to Rollins College in 1957 for use as a women's dormitory. The site is now occupied by Sutton Place South apartments.

(2) 550 Osceola Avenue

*Peckham House

A home was built here facing the lake in 1884 for Colonel Peleg Peckham of St. Louis. The house was later owned by Ray Greene, and in 1959 it was converted into apartments. After 2000, it was replaced by the Barker House, the home of the president of Rollins College.

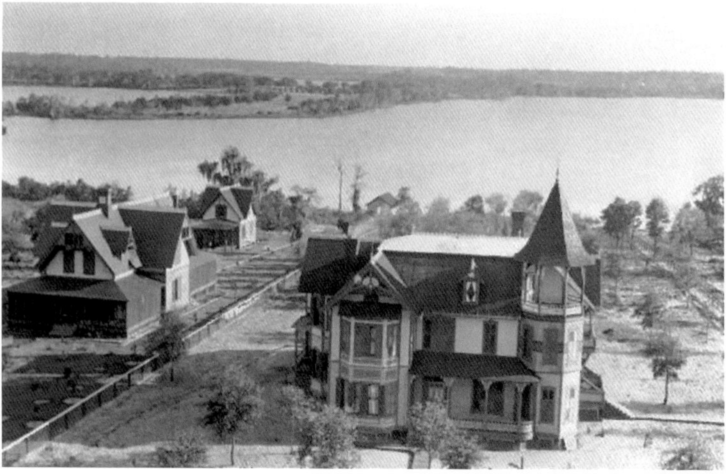

Peckham and Batchelor Houses

This 1880s view from the top of the Seminole Hotel shows two large homes just north of Lake Virginia. On the left is the Peckham House, erected in 1884. The one on the right with the hexagonal tower and conical cap was the home of Richard Batchelor. *Courtesy of the Florida Photographic Collection.*

Continue east on Osceola Avenue and head south on Henkel Circle and south on Genius Drive to the gate crossing the road.

(3) 930 Genius Drive

Wind Song

In 1951, Hugh and Jeannette Genius McKean moved into Wind Song, a home that Richard Genius had built along Genius Drive. It sits on a portion of a 150-acre parcel that had been owned by Jeannette's grandfather, Charles Morse. It can be visited by land only with prior permission to enter this gated community, and it can be viewed along the Scenic Boat Tour.

Walk north on Genius Drive.

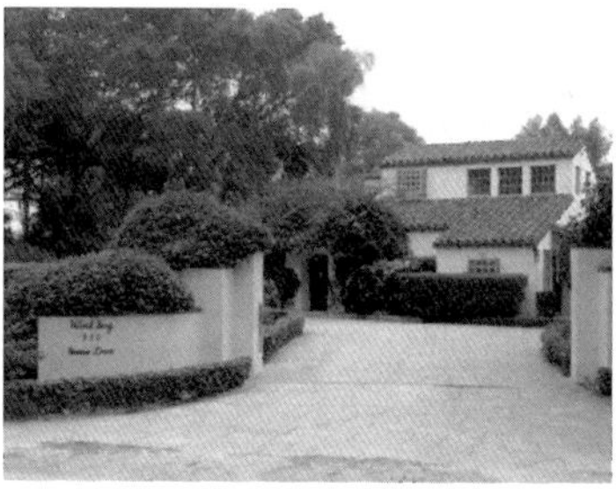

Wind Song

This residence of Hugh and Jeannette McKean is also known as Villa Genius. It is located on Genius Drive and was built by Richard Genius. It features a red tile roof, a fountain with decorative tile imported from Spain and iron grillwork. *Courtesy of the Florida Photographic Collection.*

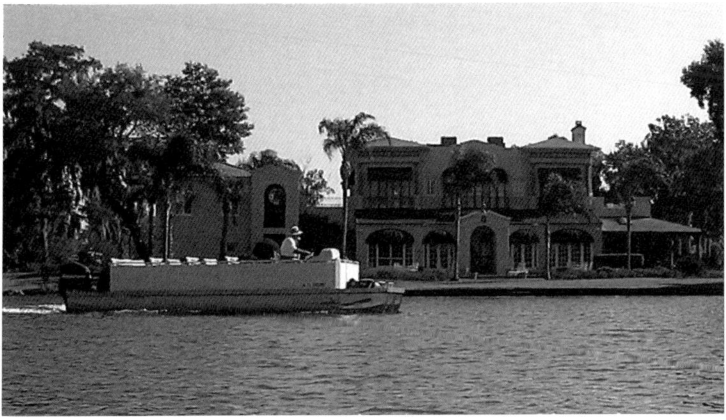

MARTIN HALL
This large home faces two lakes, and its address is on Genius Drive, just across a narrow strip of land from Lake Mizell. The back of the house shown here commands a magnificent view of Lake Virginia. Also shown in the image is one of the Scenic Boat Tour pontoon boats taking a pair of passengers to see the sites. *Photo by Steve Rajtar.*

(4) 1000 GENIUS DRIVE

MARTIN HALL

The Business Men's Club had this home built in the early 1920s as the club's headquarters. That use was brief, as the home was sold for $85,000 in 1925 to W.R. Rynlander. In 1930, he sold it to John and Prestonia Martin, who were assisted by artist Sam Stoltz in its remodeling. Dr. Martin was an international relations consultant and conference leader at Rollins College, and after his death in 1956, the Mediterranean-style mansion became known as Martin Hall. The college acquired it as its Conservatory of Music, sold it in 1976 and it has been privately owned since.

Continue north on Genius Drive and head north (right) on Henkel Circle and northeast on Osceola Avenue. When the road curves to the north, continue eastward on the sidewalk, which connects to another section of Osceola. Continue east on the sidewalk and Grove Terrace.

(5) 1401 GROVE TERRACE

GRISWOLD-WARD COTTAGE

Charles H. Ward of Vermont and his son, Harold A. Ward, moved to Winter Park in 1886 and became involved in growing citrus. After the Big Freeze, the Wards brought several groves back into production and acquired this home on the south shore of Lake Sylvan, formerly the residence of Holland A. Griswold.

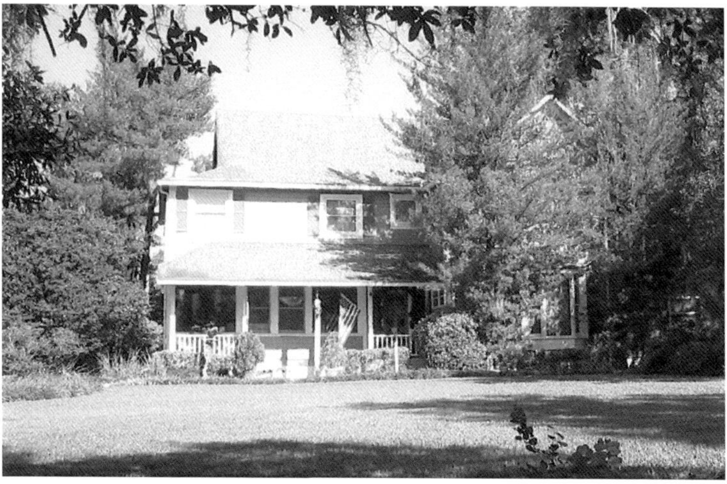

GRISWOLD-WARD COTTAGE
This home has been modified several times since the Ward family acquired it in the late 1890s. Changes include the enlargement of the entrance porch on the side away from the lake and the replacement of the windows. *Photo by Gayle Prince Rajtar.*

Harold managed the properties of Charles Morse and served as the secretary of the Winter Park Land Company.

Continue east on Grove Terrace and head northeast on Harris Circle.

(6) 1554 HARRIS CIRCLE

McCALLUM-HARRIS HOUSE

This home built in an orange grove in 1887 features a trio of roof dormers. They, along with the chimney pots, provide a Tudor Gothic appearance. The home also has a shed-roofed veranda on three sides of the first story. The original wood siding has been covered by stucco.

Continue northeast on Harris Circle and walk north and east on Roundelay Lane, north on Sylvan Drive, take the right fork and continue north on Shepherd Avenue across Aloma Avenue, west on Bryan Avenue, northwest on Maiden Lane and north on Bonita Drive.

(7) 724 BONITA DRIVE

COMSTOCK-HARRIS HOUSE

This Queen Anne–style home on the east shore of Lake Osceola was built by William Comstock as his winter cottage in 1883,

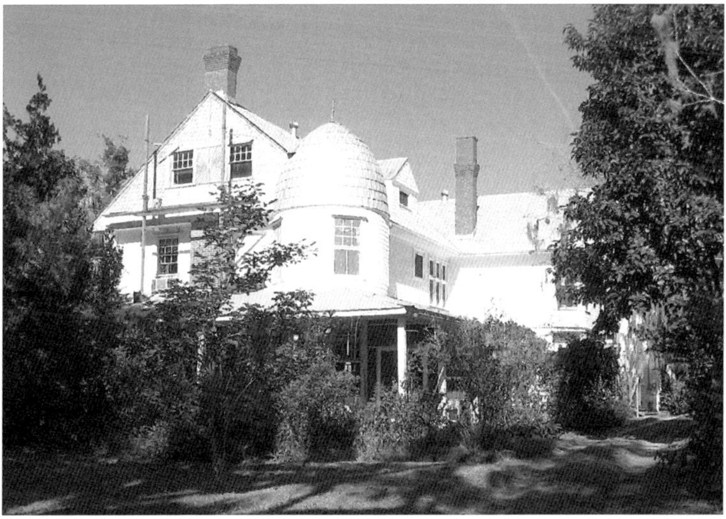

EASTBANK
This home, named for its location on the east side of Lake Osceola, was built with a shingle style. It has three stories made of wood, supported by a brick foundation. Inside, there are six fireplaces and a main staircase that turns in front of a stained-glass window. *Photo by Steve Rajtar.*

making it the oldest surviving home in Winter Park. Today's Bonita Drive began as the camphor tree–lined driveway to the house, which sat on a sixty-acre tract before it was subdivided and sold for other homesites. The home, also known as Eastbank, was added to the National Register of Historic Places in 1983.

Head south on Bonita Drive.

(8) 711 BONITA DRIVE

ORECK HOUSE

This 1935 home was designed by James Gamble Rogers II in the French Provincial style. It bears some resemblance to his own house, Four Winds, which was built in 1929 on the Isle of Sicily.

Walk southeast on Maiden Lane, west on Bryan Avenue, south on Sylvan Drive and west on Aloma Avenue.

(9) 1331 ALOMA AVENUE

WADDELL COTTAGE

William J. Waddell built this cottage on a ten-acre tract in 1897. He owned and operated a boardinghouse north of Lake Osceola known as the Osceola House, and also served as an

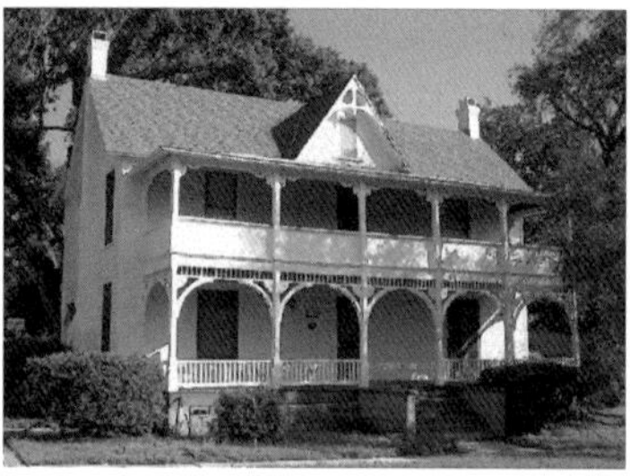

Waddell Cottage
This two-story house has Victorian details and a front porch along the entire length of both stories. It originally sat on a much larger lot, but in 1923 Carl Galloway purchased the lot and built other homes there, leaving this one with a much smaller yard. *Photo by Steve Rajtar.*

alderman and deputy marshal. The adjacent road, formerly known as Oviedo Avenue, was renamed in 1926 after Aloma Creek, which parallels it for a distance.

Continue west on Aloma Avenue and head north on Cortland Avenue and southwest on Alberta Drive.

(10) 425 Alberta Drive

Edwards-Carlton House

This was the home of Grace O. Edwards, one of the daughters of Benjamin Edwards. Grace graduated in 1894 from Wellesley College and, with her sister Helen, developed a noted garden at the home they inherited from their father at 461 East Webster Avenue. Grace moved from there in 1938, when she had this house built. She was one of the founders of the Winter Park Garden Club in 1922 and also helped to beautify the grounds of Rollins College.

Walk south on Alberta Drive, west on Lakewood Drive and south on Detmar Drive.

(11) 234 Detmar Drive

The Palms Caretaker's House

This house was built in 1910 as a seven-room home for the caretaker of The Palms. Front and back porches and a wash shed were removed, and a two-story north wing was added. Original heart pine siding, covered by aluminum on the front, can be seen on the back when the house is viewed from Brewer Avenue. The house was moved here in 1951–52.

(12) 138 Detmar Avenue

Geer–van den Berg House

Dr. Ira B. Geer, one of the town's first doctors, built this Victorian-style home in the early 1880s on a lot he had purchased from

Wilson Phelps in 1876. He used it as his office as well as his home. Originally, the porch entrance was in the middle of the front, but later it was moved to the corner and the porch was extended around the side. Also added later to the back and side were a two-story addition and a deck/gazebo.

Walk south and west on Detmar Drive and north on Trismen Terrace.

(13) 240 TRISMEN TERRACE

THE PALMS

Rollins College inherited this property upon the 1887 death of Alonzo Rollins. The groves provided income to the school until they were virtually destroyed in the Big Freeze. In 1897, Edward H. Brewer bought the land as a site for a winter cottage and built this home the following year. Originally, it was clapboard topped by a wood shingle roof and had a spindle-balustraded veranda. It was remodeled in 1924 to duplicate the Brewers' Georgian revival–style residence in Cortland, New York.

Today, the home is dominated by a colonial revival–style front, with a massive portico supported by paired columns. The interior was redesigned in 1937–38 by James Gamble Rogers II for then-owner Frederick Trismen. In 1979, the home was acquired by marijuana dealer Robert W. Govern. In 1982, he was convicted of drug trafficking and was sentenced to forty-five

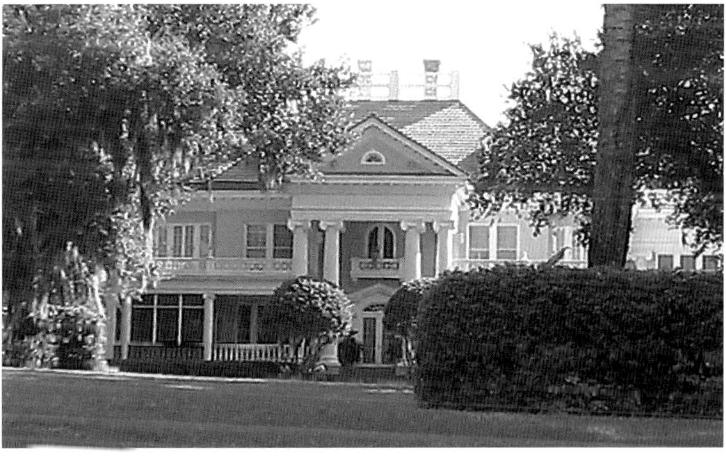

THE PALMS

The front of this mansion faces Lake Osceola rather than a road, so few people, other than Scenic Boat Tour passengers, ever see it. It was built on forty acres, but all but five were sold by the Trismens in 1951 to be subdivided it into the Detmar Terrace and Osceola Shores subdivisions. *Photo by Steve Rajtar.*

years in prison, and federal authorities confiscated the home. The mansion stood vacant and then was sold by the government to Roy and Patricia Ambinder in 1987, five years after it was added to the National Register of Historic Places.

Head south on Trismen Terrace and west on Osceola Avenue.

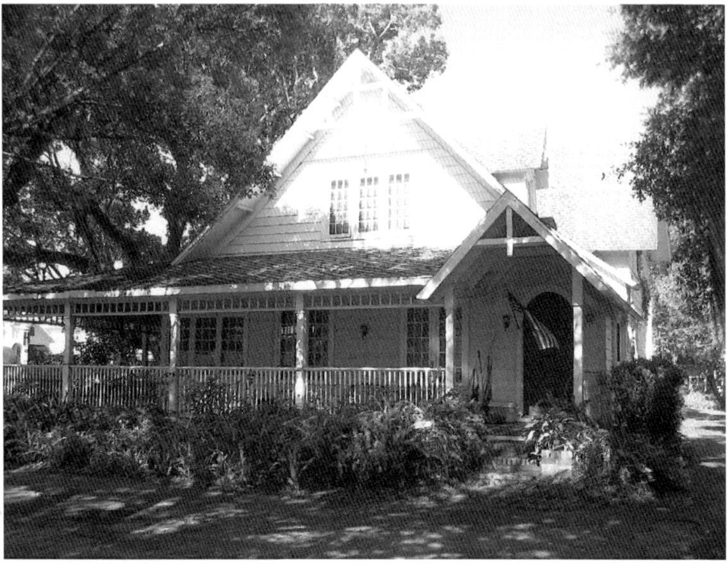

WARD COTTAGE
Next to the sidewalk in front of the house is a bronze tablet commemorating its use in 1885–86 as the first women's dormitory for Rollins College. This house is nicknamed "The Camphors" for its large camphor trees, some of which can be seen here. *Photo by Gayle Prince Rajtar.*

(14) 621 OSCEOLA AVENUE

WARD COTTAGE

This home was built in 1883 by Reverend Charles W. Ward, the minister who presided over the first Episcopal service in Winter Park on April 15 of that year. On the Osceola Court side are two large camphor trees framing a view of the multiple gables and narrow, banded windows. Mrs. Ward died in 1884, and after selling the home to Alonzo Rollins, Reverend Ward moved to New Jersey and committed suicide.

Continue west on Osceola Avenue and head south on Ollie Avenue to the beginning of the tour.

Northern Winter Park

Site	Miles	Address	Site	Miles	Address
1	0.0	1363 Alabama Dr.	13	3.0	740–800 Palmer Ave.
2	0.2	1600 Alabama Dr.	14	3.4	915 Old England Ave.
3	0.3	1700 Alabama Dr.	15	3.5	876 Old England Ave.
4	0.3	1411 Via Tuscany	16	3.6	461 E. Webster Ave.
5	0.4	1461 Via Tuscany	17	3.7	253 E. Webster Ave.
6	1.2	1 Isle of Sicily	18	4.2	155 W. Stovin Ave.
7	1.2	2 Isle of Sicily	19	4.2	173 W. Stovin Ave.
8	2.6	701 Via Bella	20	4.7	1300 Summerland Ave.
9	2.8	1020 Palmer Ave.	21	5.1	1290 N. Park Ave.
10	2.8	950 Palmer Ave.	22	5.1	1280 N. Park Ave.
11	2.8	916 Palmer Ave.	23	5.6	1200 N. Park Ave.
12	3.0	800 Palmer Ave.	24	6.2	225 Palmer Ave.
				6.9	End

Begin at Kraft Azalea Gardens, which can be reached from Palmer Avenue by driving north on Alabama Drive.

(1) 1363 Alabama Drive

Kraft Memorial Azalea Gardens

In 1937, Honor Azalea Gardens was renamed Kraft Memorial Azalea Gardens in memory of George Kraft. In 1939, a stone and plaque monument was erected within the park to honor Judge Leonard J. Hackney as the creator of the gardens.

Walk east on Alabama Drive.

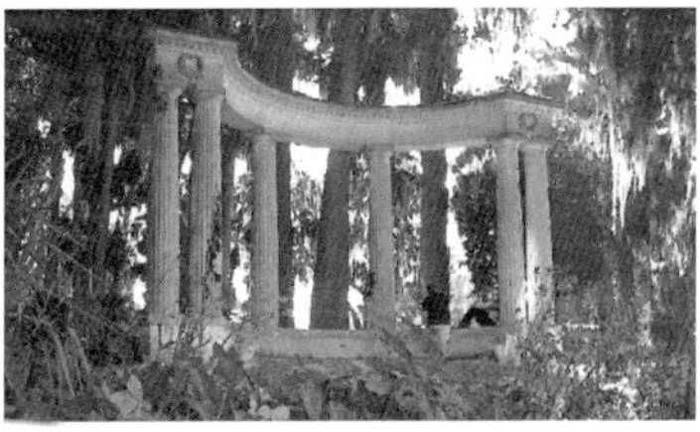

KRAFT MEMORIAL AZALEA GARDENS

In the park is this large, columned monument, which is inscribed "Pause Friend let beauty refresh the spirit." It was given to the city in 1969 by Kenneth H. and Elizabeth P. Kraft in memory of George and Maud H. Kraft, and it is a popular venue for weddings. *Photo by Steve Rajtar.*

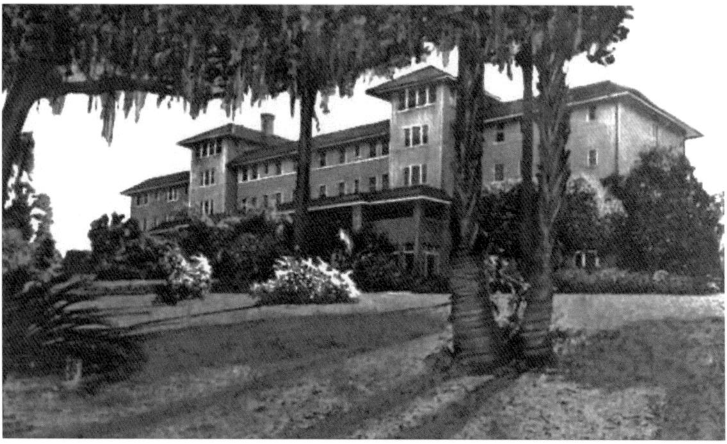

ALABAMA HOTEL
Constructed in 1921–22 as a traditional hotel, it was operated as such until 1960, when it became the Mayell-Alabama Retirement Hotel. In 1979, it was converted by Charles Booth and Charles Simmerson to condominium apartments. *Courtesy of the Florida Photographic Collection.*

(2) 1600 ALABAMA DRIVE

ALABAMA HOTEL

This land was sold by William C. Temple in 1915. In 1921, Joseph Kronenberger began construction on a four-story, eighty-room hotel that he hoped would attract Northern visitors. It was completed in 1922 and leased in 1923 to D.L. Rice and F.B. Lynch. Later, it was sold to Fred and Clifford Folger, who lost it during the Great Depression. Next door to the west is the Temple Refectory, which Temple built in 1904 as a summer kitchen and dining room adjacent to his house. It has a full basement, so it was not moved with the house when the hotel was built. The refectory was converted to a clubhouse for the Alabama Condominiums.

(3) 1700 ALABAMA DRIVE

TEMPLE HOUSE

This Florida Victorian–style home was built in 1878 a little to the west on the present site of the Alabama Hotel. It had originally been owned by the Packwood family, and later by the Palmers, and then was acquired by William and Carrie Temple. They added a private gas plant and a sewage system and, in 1912, a telephone. Well water was routed in pipes to the five bathrooms.

Head north on Via Tuscany.

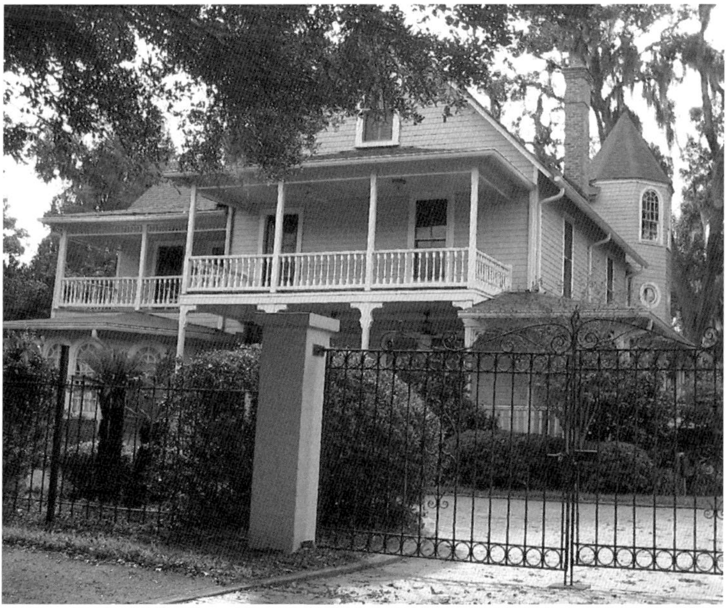

TEMPLE HOUSE
This was the home of William Temple, owner of the Willcardo Fruit Company, growers and shippers of Florida citrus. Temple's local groves were known as the Sunnyside and the Alabama, which was also the name he gave to this house built in 1870. *Photo by Gayle Prince Rajtar.*

(4) 1411 VIA TUSCANY

MACCAUGHEY-TAYLOR HOUSE

This house was built by Andrew B. MacCaughey of Chicago in about 1925. He spent twenty Florida winters in it. The style is Mediterranean, with white stucco and a breezeway connecting the main house and the guesthouse/servants' quarters. Some of the details, including the stone fireplace and mantel, come from prior designs by architect Addison Mizner. The exterior underwent a major renovation in 2007–08.

Continue north on Via Tuscany.

(5) 1461 VIA TUSCANY

SANDSCOVE

This Georgian revival home, also known as Cloister Groves, was built in the Italianate villa style in 1918–19 by James Stokes. At the time, it was the focal point of a five-acre tract that included citrus groves.

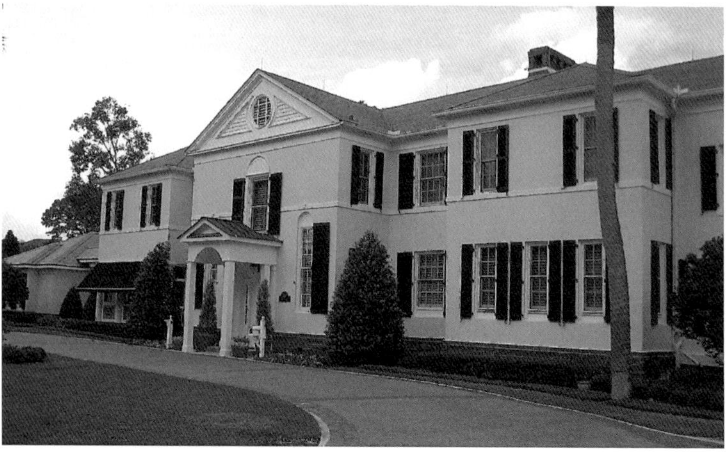

SANDSCOVE
The original owner of this home was James Stokes of Connecticut, who died before he could move in. His large tract of land included an entrance drive that began to the east at Lake Knowles and led up to the front door. *Photo by Gayle Prince Rajtar.*

Continue north on Via Tuscany and head west on Via Lugano across the bridge.

(6) 1 ISLE OF SICILY

*BURRESS HOUSE

Located here was the second home built on the Isle of Sicily, designed by James Gamble Rogers II in 1936 for Paul Burress. He took a Spanish-style plan and incorporated into it the half-timbering of an English country cottage. The roof was covered with flat terra cotta tiles and the home was connected by a loggia to a studio and garage. A longtime owner was John M. Tiedtke, the Rollins College treasurer and business manager beginning in 1948. It was replaced by newer construction in 2007.

(7) 2 ISLE OF SICILY

HAUCK-BOLEN HOUSE

A mining engineer who worked with Albert Einstein on the Manhattan Project, Frederick A. Hauck of Cincinnati for many years wintered in this home. It was acquired by James L. and Phyllis G. Bolen in 1978, and they remain its owners.

Head east on Via Lugano, south on Temple Drive (to the right around Lake Knowles), west on Palmer Avenue and south on Via Bella.

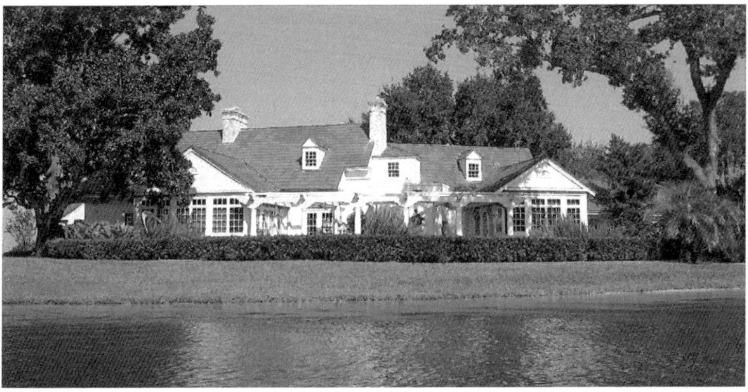

HAUCK-BOLEN HOUSE
This home was designed by James Gamble Rogers II, who lived next door. This home has a gross square footage of more than 13,700, less than half of which consists of air-conditioned and heated living areas. *Photo by Steve Rajtar.*

(8) 701 VIA BELLA

GUILD HOUSE

Pharmacist Dr. William A. Guild of Boston built this sixteen-room home on eighteen acres and operated it as a boardinghouse called the Osceola House.

Walk north on Via Bella and west on Palmer Avenue.

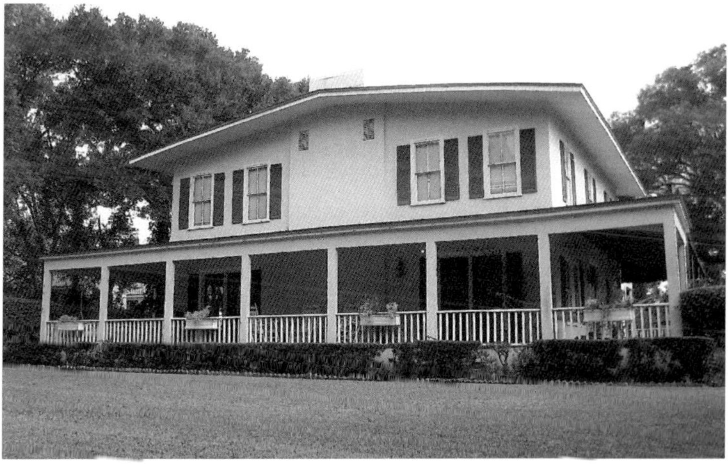

GUILD HOUSE
This property was abandoned, probably in 1895 right after the Big Freeze, and was acquired by Mr. and Mrs. Frank Spooner in 1905. They renovated it and renamed it Weatogue, meaning "wigwam place." *Photo by Gayle Prince Rajtar.*

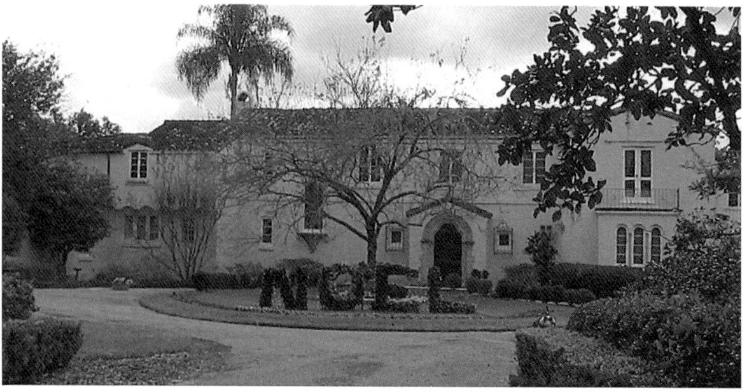

MERRYWOOD
This home was designed by James Gamble Rogers II, who also handled modifications for owner George S. Marsh. There is a two-story extension at its western end, featuring round-headed windows on the first story, but during the 1980s Rogers stated that this addition was not part of his designs. *Photo by Gayle Prince Rajtar.*

(9) 1020 PALMER AVENUE

MERRYWOOD

This home was designed in 1938 by James Gamble Rogers II for Caroline Plant of Massachusetts. The Spanish eclectic–style home has typical buff-colored stucco and a red tile roof. It was the largest home designed by Rogers, at almost seven thousand square feet. Upon the death of Mrs. Plant, the home was sold and her estate was distributed to charitable organizations, including Rollins College.

Continue west on Palmer Avenue.

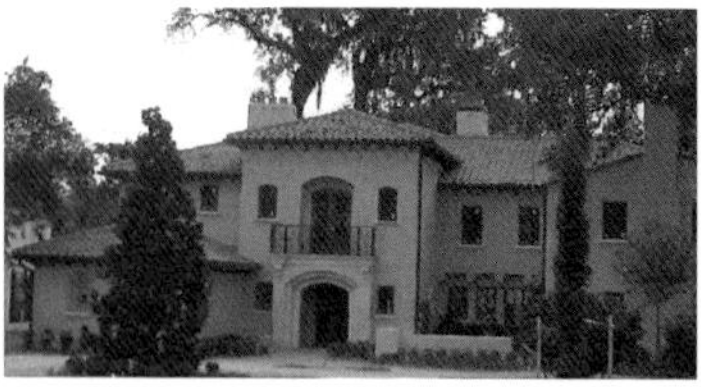

CHASE-SCHENCK HOUSE
This home originally had about 3,700 square feet of living space and was built in a Spanish style with buff-colored stucco and a red tile roof. During 2007–08, it underwent a substantial remodeling. *Photo by Gayle Prince Rajtar.*

(10) 950 PALMER AVENUE

CHASE-SCHENCK HOUSE

Joshua C. Chase built this house in 1926 with a design similar to those developed by James Gamble Rogers II, but the architect's participation has not been confirmed. The Spanish-style home has buff-colored stucco and a red tile roof. The Jay E. Schenck family later owned it.

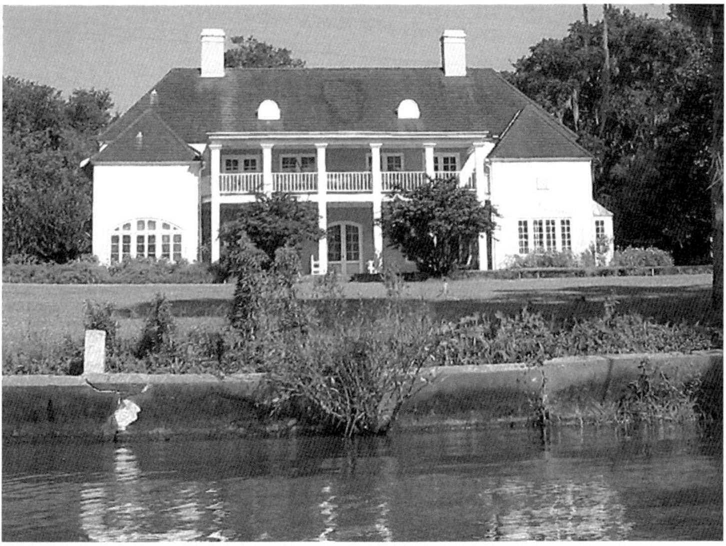

CARLOVA
This is a view from Lake Osceola of the large English Tudor–style home dating to 1915. Its unusual name comes from portions of names of three states: Carolina, Ohio and Virginia. *Photo by Steve Rajtar.*

(11) 916 PALMER AVENUE

CARLOVA

Dr. H.W. Caldwell had this home built by Hanner Brothers in 1914–15. During 1936, Woodbury T. Morris purchased it and had James Gamble Rogers II redesign the exterior in a French style, including the addition of a two-story wing on the northeast corner.

(12) 800 PALMER AVENUE

CODDINGTON HOUSE

James Gamble Rogers II designed this home in 1941 for C.A. Coddington. For much of its existence, it was painted white and the shutters were dark green, a combination that went well with the red tile roof. It was also known for its impressive landscaping. Later owners include Jon and Carolyn McMillan.

(13) BETWEEN 740 AND 800 PALMER AVENUE

CANAL BRIDGE

This bridge was erected in 1924 by the Luton Bridge Company of York, Pennsylvania. The first permanent bridge over the

Maitland Run, before it was dug out as a canal, had been erected in 1888 for $355 by Capen & Company.

Continue west on Palmer Avenue and head south on Old England Avenue.

(14) 915 OLD ENGLAND AVENUE

LEONARD HOUSE

This is the only international-style home designed by James Gamble Rogers II. He prepared its plans in 1937 for Mr. and Mrs. Edgar C. Leonard. His design included ribbon windows, a terrace on the flat roof and asymmetrical facades. In 1997, the home was substantially remodeled to take on a more Mediterranean appearance.

(15) 876 OLD ENGLAND AVENUE

STEINWAY HOUSE

This home was built in 1936–37 for Mrs. Steinway of the piano manufacturing family. It was designed by James Gamble Rogers II in a typical New England style, with a simple pediment over the front door.

Continue south on Old England Avenue and head east on Webster Avenue.

(16) 461 EAST WEBSTER AVENUE

EDWARDS HOUSE

Benjamin Edwards built this craftsman-style home in 1915 on land that was formerly a citrus grove. It has a full basement and attic. The screened porch on the east side is original; the one on the north was added later. The house is known to some as Orchard Place.

Walk west on Webster Avenue.

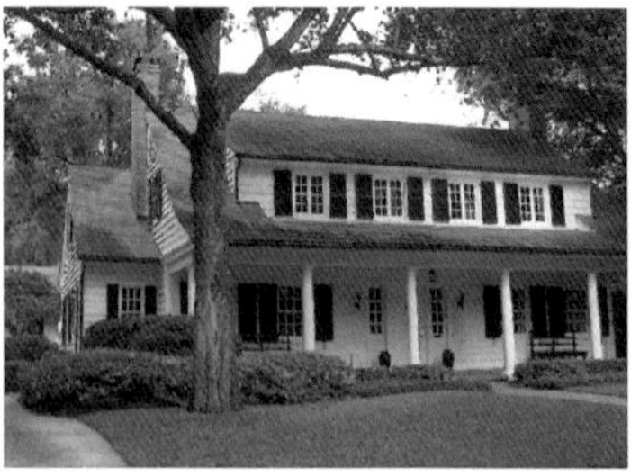

EDWARDS HOUSE
This home, which dates to 1915, was inherited by the original owner's daughters, Helen and Grace Edwards. It was later owned by William Foster, who served as a Rollins College trustee. *Photo by Gayle Prince Rajtar.*

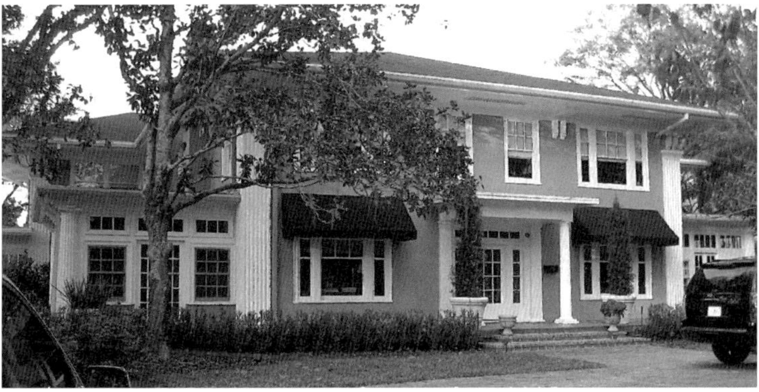

PHILLIPS HOUSE
This home displays Georgian features, including a rectangular block form, hip roof, corner pilasters, a substantial portico and a total sense of symmetry. Eave brackets show a nineteenth-century Victorian influence. *Photo by Gayle Prince Rajtar.*

(17) 253 EAST WEBSTER AVENUE

PHILLIPS HOUSE

This is an example of a Georgian revival–style residence, uncommon in Winter Park. At the time this architectural movement was flourishing, Winter Park's population was declining because of the freezes of 1894–95. This was built in about 1905 for E.R. Phillips.

Continue west on Webster Avenue and head north on Park Avenue and west on Stovin Avenue.

(18) 155 WEST STOVIN AVENUE

CALDWELL-STRONG HOUSE

This home was built in the late 1930s for the first dean of Knowles Memorial Chapel, Charles A. Campbell. The eastern and western wings, including a two-car garage and living quarters, are later additions.

Continue west on Stovin Avenue.

(19) 173 WEST STOVIN AVENUE

WAGNER-SHANNON COTTAGE

This is a simple 1920s retirement bungalow with a view of the golf course. It was the home of Bert Wagner and his wife Rachael Wallace, and later was the home of their daughter Jean Shannon and her husband Earl.

Continue west on Stovin Avenue and head north on New York Avenue, west on Park Avenue and north on Summerland Avenue.

(20) 1300 Summerland Avenue

Lawrence-Chubb Cottage

Henry S. Chubb moved to Winter Park from Vermont in 1880 and planted a citrus grove for Colonel Franklin Fairbanks in an area now known as the Eastgate subdivision. The Chubbs lived in a log cabin at the corner of Phelps and Aloma Avenues, and in 1899 they bought this home on the south shore of Lake Maitland. It was built in 1883 for shoe manufacturer Judge Lewis H. Lawrence of New York.

Head south on Summerland Avenue, east on Park Avenue and north on New York Avenue.

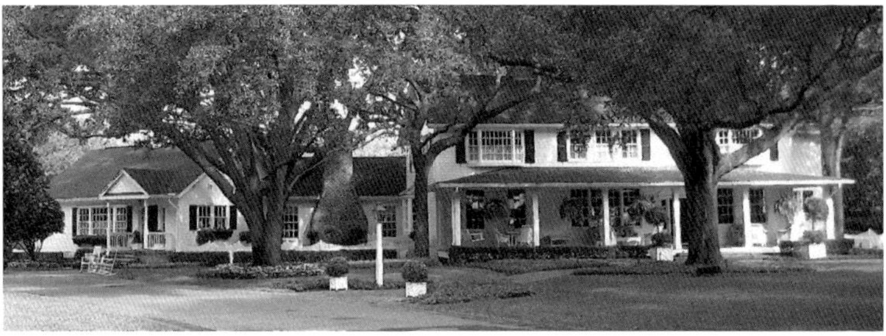

Lawrence-Chubb Cottage
This home has a Federal-style entrance, an unusual trait for a Central Florida residence. When it was built in 1883, its grounds consisted of ten acres, much of which was planted with citrus that was damaged by the Big Freeze. *Photo by Gayle Prince Rajtar.*

(21) 1290 North Park Avenue

Shippen House

Unitarian minister Eugene Shippen and his wife Elizabeth moved to Winter Park in 1930 and the following year this home was built for them. It features an engaged chimney pot, a cantilevered balcony, a *U*-shaped courtyard, textured stucco on thick walls and an intentional sag in the roofline to simulate age.

Walk south on New York Avenue.

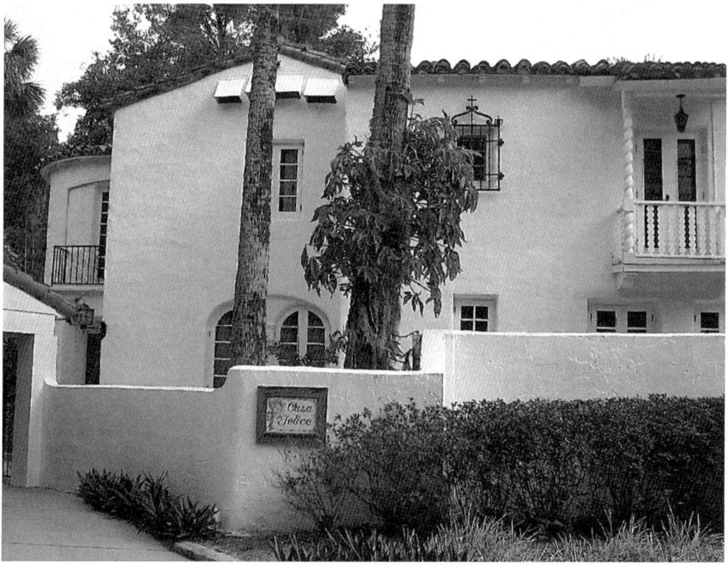

SHIPPEN HOUSE
This was the residence of Dr. and Mrs. Shippen, who named it Casa Felice, meaning "house of happiness." They hired James Gamble Rogers II to design it in 1931, and this was his first project with a Spanish eclectic style. *Photo by Gayle Prince Rajtar.*

(22) 1280 NORTH PARK AVENUE

JEWETT HOUSE

Art moderne in style, this home was designed by James Gamble Rogers II in 1937 for Eugene L. and Zoe Jewett. Unlike the better-known Rogers homes with Spanish appearances, this home has glass blocks, a flat roof and curved corners. Jewett established a local orthopedic practice that continues today. The Jewetts called their home Tree Tops and lived in it for only four years before they divorced.

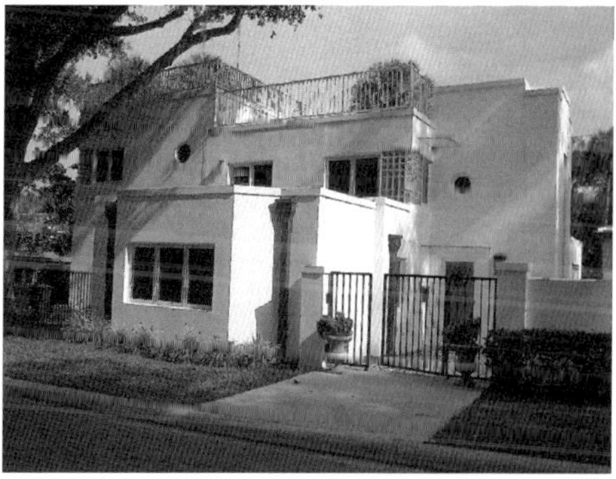

JEWETT HOUSE
Although showing a very different style, this home has a close relationship with the Shippen House next door. When this was built, Zoe Jewett lived here and her parents lived next door. In 1997, this house was acquired by the owners of the neighboring house. *Photo by Gayle Prince Rajtar.*

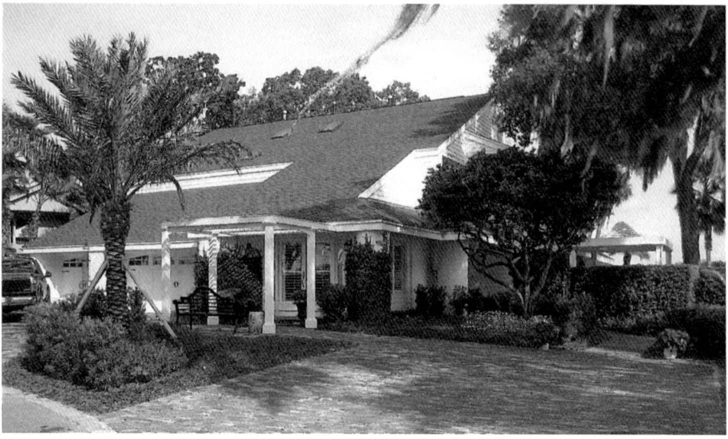

Twelve Oaks
This house was built in 1956 at a cost of $150,000. Hollow clay walls are covered with stucco and have a very modern appearance. A solarium overlooks Lake Maitland. The home was designed by James Gamble Rogers II. *Courtesy of the Florida Photographic Collection.*

(23) 1200 North Park Avenue

Twelve Oaks

This winter home on Lake Maitland was the residence of Archibald Granville Bush, the chairman of the board of the Minnesota Mining and Manufacturing Company. He and his wife Edyth built the home in 1949.

Head southeast on Park Avenue and east on Palmer Avenue.

(24) 225 Palmer Avenue

Mizener House

This Georgian colonial revival–style home designed by James Gamble Rogers II was built in 1936–39 for Mildred W. Mizener of Pennsylvania. It was constructed of concrete block covered with stucco, cost $35,000 and was designed for entertaining large groups.

Continue east on Palmer Avenue and head north and east on Alabama Drive to the beginning of the tour.

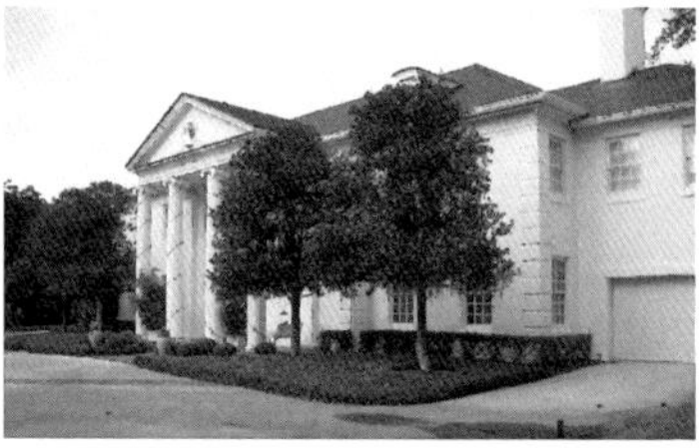

Mizener House
In the late 1930s, Mildred Mizener complicated things for the firm of James Gamble Rogers II. She inserted herself in the design process to eliminate elements she felt were not essential. For example, she vetoed window shutters because she did not want to have to paint them. *Photo by Gayle Prince Rajtar.*

Rollins College

Site	Miles	Name	Site	Miles	Name
1	0.1	Sutton Place South	29	1.4	Cross Hall
2	0.2	Holt Hall	30	1.4	Mayflower Hall
3	0.3	Faculty Monument	31	1.4	Pugsley Hall
4	0.3	Crummer Hall (back)	32	1.5	Beal-Maltbie Center
5	0.3	Bush Executive Center	33	1.5	Alumni House
6	0.3	Bush Science Center	34	1.5	Rice Family Bookstore
7	0.4	Barker Family Stadium	35	1.5	Carnegie Hall
8	0.5	Cahall-Sandspur Field	36	1.5	Nelson Rose Garden
9	0.5	McKean Gateway	37	1.5	Warren Admin. Building
10	0.6	Rinker Building	38	1.5	Walk of Fame
11	0.7	College Arms	39	1.6	Mills Memorial Center
12	0.7	Casa Iberia	40	1.6	Chase Hall
13	0.7	Hauck Hall	41	1.7	Pinehurst Hall
14	0.8	Strong Hall	42	1.7	Gale Hall
15	0.8	Corrin Hall	43	1.7	Lyman Hall
16	0.8	Elizabeth Hall	44	1.7	Knowles Memorial Chapel
17	0.8	Fox Hall	45	1.7	Hooker Hall
18	0.9	Ward Hall	46	1.8	Rollins Hall
19	1.0	French House	47	1.9	McKean Hall
20	1.1	Orlando Hall	48	1.9	Alfond Boathouse
21	1.1	Olin Library	49	2.0	Cornell Art Center
22	1.1	Cornell Campus Center	50	2.0	Cornell Fine Arts Museum
23	1.1	Alfond Swimming Pool	51	2.0	Rex Beach Hall
24	1.2	Woolson House	52	2.1	Keene Hall
25	1.2	Sullivan House	53	2.1	Annie Russell Theatre
26	1.3	Mary Jean Mitchell Plaza	54	2.1	Alfond Sports Center
27	1.3	Tiedtke Tennis Courts	55	2.1	Cornell Hall
28	1.4	Dyer Memorial	56	2.2	Fred Stone Theatre
				2.4	End

Begin on Ollie Avenue (a block south of Fairbanks Avenue), adjacent to the park at Dinky Dock. Walk north on Ollie to the intersection with Fairbanks.

(1) SUTTON PLACE SOUTH

These apartments are owned and operated by the college for upper classmen and new transfer students seeking a quiet, studious atmosphere. Students are carefully screened and must meet standards, including a grade-point average threshold.

Walk southwest and west on the south side of Fairbanks Avenue.

(2) HOLT HALL

Hamilton Holt Hall is a coed residence hall with male students on the first floor and offers separate bathroom facilities for men and women. New students make up about one-third of its population.

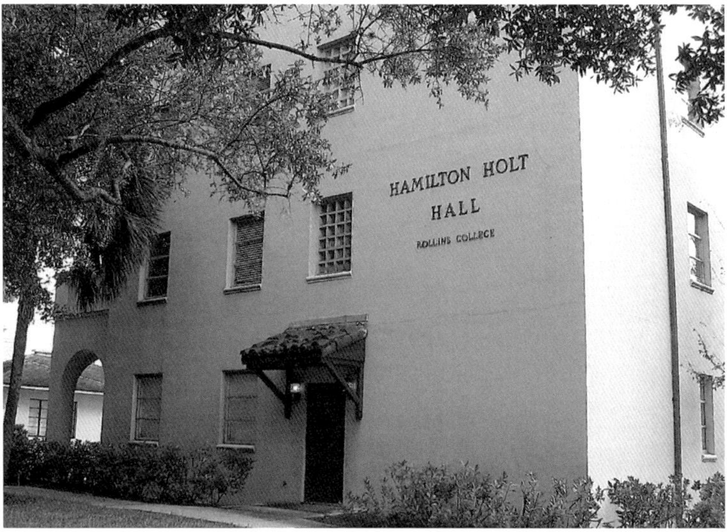

HOLT HALL
Hamilton Holt Hall was built in 1966 for use as a dormitory and was named in honor of the college's eighth president. Holt is credited with establishing the Spanish Mediterranean style of architecture found throughout the campus. *Photo by Gayle Prince Rajtar.*

(3) FACULTY MONUMENT

This bronze plaque set in a large coquina rock was placed here by the faculty in 1935 to commemorate the fiftieth anniversary of the first meeting of the initial faculty of Rollins College held on November 2, 1885.

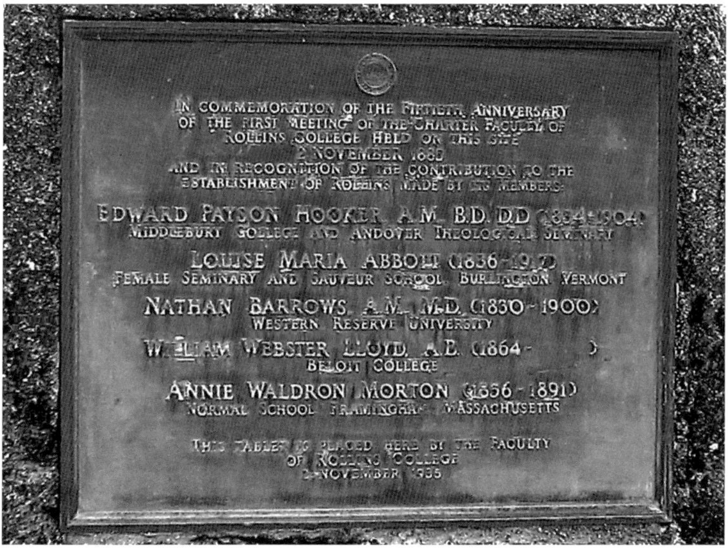

FACULTY MONUMENT

This monument commemorates the college's first faculty, consisting of Edward P. Hooker, Louise M. Abbott, Nathan Barrows, William W. Lloyd and Annie W. Morton. *Photo by Gayle Prince Rajtar.*

(4) CRUMMER HALL (BACK)

Roy E. Crummer, a former Kansas bond agent who helped restore Florida's economy in 1929, created an endowment in 1964 to establish the Roy E. Crummer School of Finance and Business Administration, which became exclusively a graduate school. Crummer Hall was designed by James Gamble Rogers II and was completed in 1966.

(5) BUSH EXECUTIVE CENTER

The Bush Executive Center was built in 1999 under the guidance of George H. Herbst, vice-president and treasurer. Funding included a large donation by the Edyth Bush Charitable Foundation established by the wife of Archibald Bush.

(6) BUSH SCIENCE CENTER

Archibald Bush was a Rollins trustee by 1952 and donated $800,000 to establish the science center after making a sizable contribution to the Roy E. Crummer School of Business Administration.

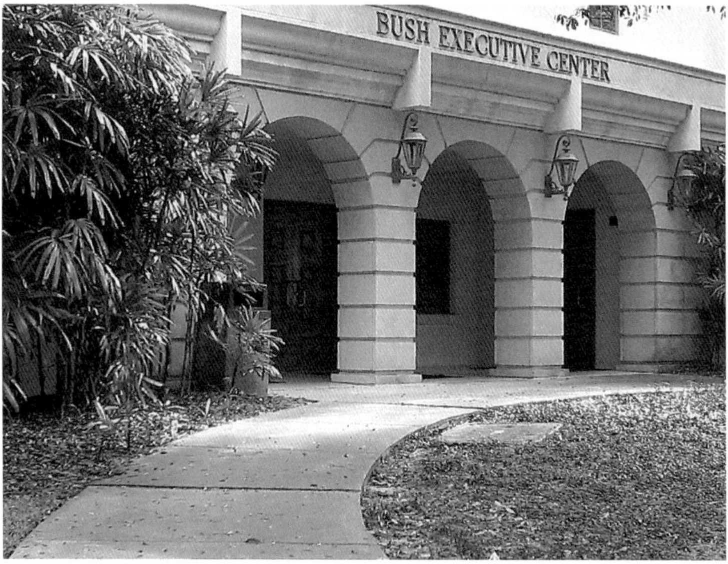

BUSH EXECUTIVE CENTER
This facility houses the Crummer Graduate School of Business and the Rollins College Corporate University, which combines the expertise of business instructors and local corporate executives to devise the curriculum for business students. *Photo by Gayle Prince Rajtar.*

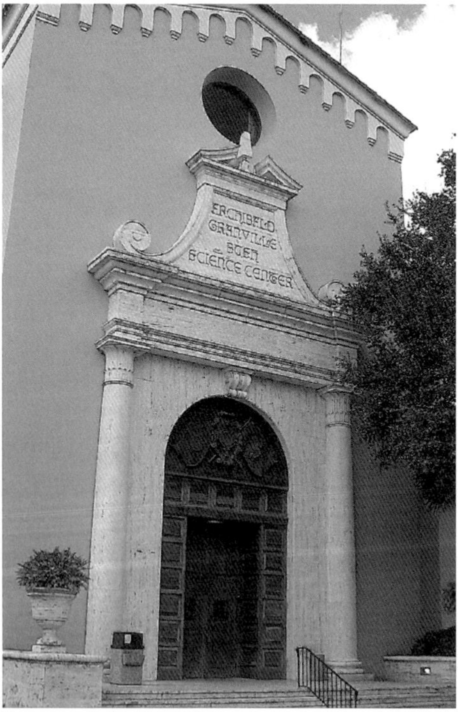

BUSH SCIENCE CENTER
The dedication of the Archibald Granville Bush Science Center took place on February 21, 1969. James Gamble Rogers II designed the building to be consistent with the Mediterranean style used throughout the campus. *Photo by Gayle Prince Rajtar.*

(7) BARKER FAMILY STADIUM

Francis H. Barker, a gifted athlete who still holds the school record for the most points scored in a basketball game, graduated from Rollins in 1952. His wife, Daryl Stamm Barker, graduated the following year. Their donations include the Barker Flagpole, Daryl's Fitness Center, the Barker Lobby of the Bush Executive Center and the Barker Family Stadium at Cahall-Sandspur Field, dedicated in 2004.

(8) CAHALL-SANDSPUR FIELD

The former community athletic field at Rollins College was named the Sandspur Bowl because of the large number of sandspurs growing there. Students and faculty raised money to light the field in 1987, and it was renovated and enlarged in 2002–04.

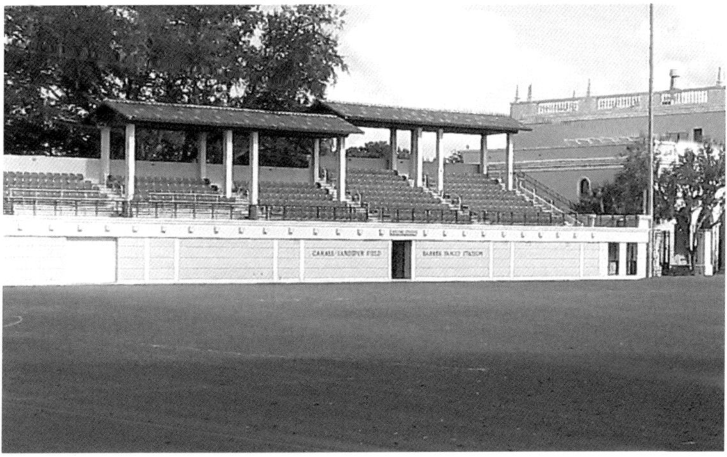

CAHALL-SANDSPUR FIELD
Peter Cahall graduated from Rollins in 1971 and helped lead the soccer team to its first appearance in the NCAA regional championship game in 1970. An active donor to The Rollins Fund, Cahall provided funds for the renovation of Sandspur Field, which was renamed to honor him. *Photo by Cayle Prince Rajtar.*

(9) MCKEAN GATEWAY

For years, Rollins was in need of a more distinctive, formal entrance to the campus. In 2002, in conjunction with a city program to rejuvenate Park Avenue, Rollins made the city an interest-free $225,000 loan that coincided with the construction of the gateway, named for the tenth president, Hugh McKean.

(10) Marshall & Vera Lee Rinker Building

The Rinker Building was the second phase of the project to provide the college with a formal entrance. Funds were provided by the M.E. Rinker Foundation, a philanthropic organization that creates endowments for education, religion and the arts. Inside are admission and financial aid offices.

Head west on Fairbanks Avenue and south on New York Avenue.

(11) College Arms

The College Arms was built in 1935 for Mrs. Gordon Jones, who became the president of the Winter Park Garden Club in 1937. The apartment house was eventually acquired by the college.

Walk east on Holt Avenue.

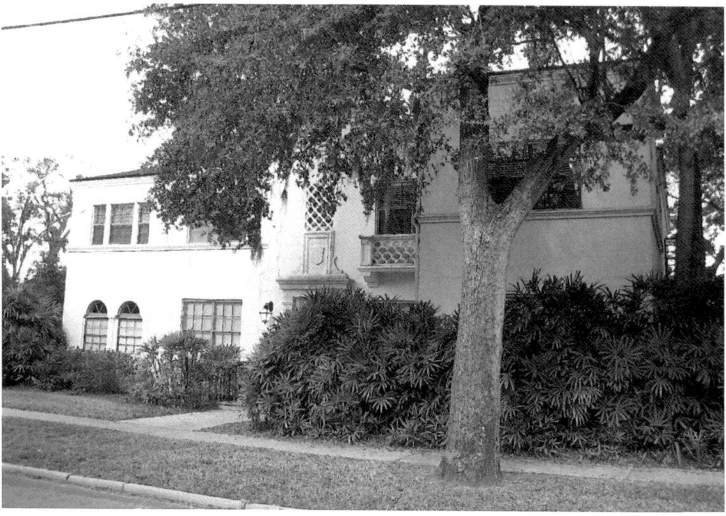

College Arms
D. Harold Hair designed the College Arms, which contains four apartments. There are two two-bedroom and two one-bedroom units, each with a living room, kitchen, bathroom and a glassed-in sun porch. *Photo by Gayle Prince Rajtar.*

(12) Casa Iberia

Casa Iberia was founded in 1942 as part of the national Good Neighbor Policy and opened in 1944 as a center for Hispanic and Inter-American Studies. Professors Alfred J. Hanna and Angela Paloma Campbell were instrumental in its establishment.

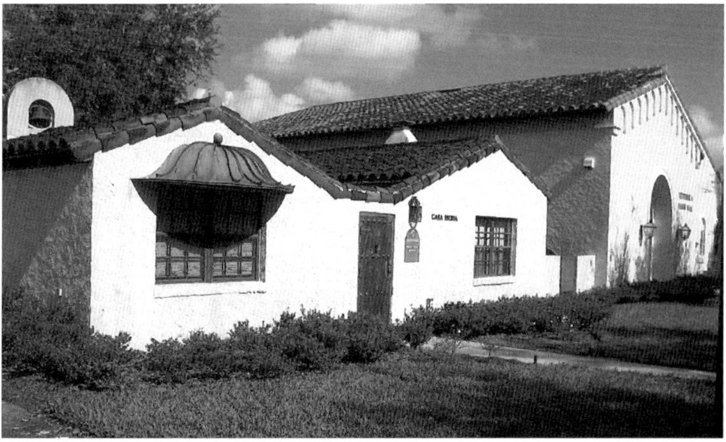

CASA IBERIA

In the 1950s and 1960s, Casa Iberia was used by students as a sanctuary for studying. After a time as an administrative center, it was rededicated in 2002 for its original use as a center for Hispanic and Inter-American studies. *Photo by Gayle Prince Rajtar.*

(13) HAUCK HALL

Frederick Hauck, a noted mineralogist and metallurgist, also worked on the development of the Sabin polio vaccine. He was a patron of cultural and educational institutions, and in 1968 he donated the Collins House, which was torn down in 1973 and replaced with this annex to Casa Iberia named in his honor.

Cross Holt Avenue.

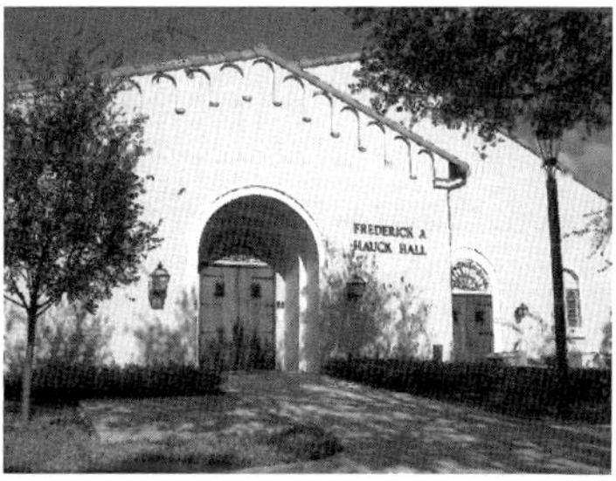

HAUCK HALL

Hauck Hall is composed of classrooms and offices for the language arts program, plus a 132-seat auditorium. It was designed by George A. Tuttle to match the Spanish Mediterranean style of the campus. *Photo by Gayle Prince Rajtar..*

(14) STRONG HALL

Harriet Corrin Strong was the widow of Henry Strong, the first president of the Eastman Kodak Company. She established the Hattie M. Strong Foundation, which provided funding for the construction of Strong Hall in 1939.

Head south on Alfred J. Hanna Way.

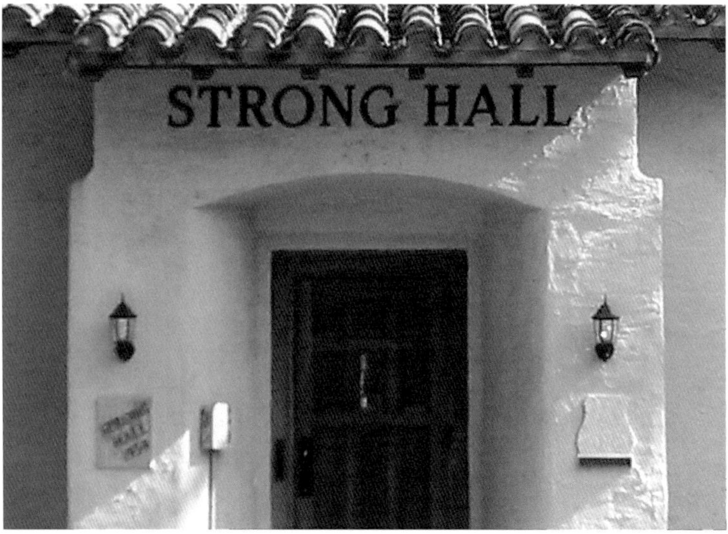

STRONG HALL
Richard Kiehnel designed several campus buildings, including Strong Hall, which currently houses the Alpha Tau Omega fraternity. The interior was originally furnished with authentic pieces in the Spanish Mediterranean style. *Photo by Gayle Prince Rajtar.*

(15) CORRIN HALL

Funding for Corrin Hall was provided by Harriet Corrin Strong to honor her son, L. Corrin Strong, a trustee during the Holt administration and an ambassador to Norway.

Walk east on the driveway and sidewalk south of Corrin Hall.

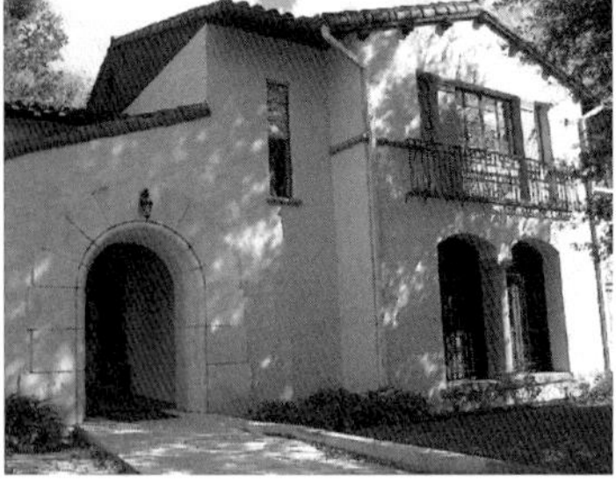

CORRIN HALL
Corrin Hall was designed by George H. Spohn with a Mediterranean theme and was built in 1946. It is currently the home of the Chi Omega sorority and fronts on Alfred J. Hanna Way, which was named for a 1917 Rollins graduate, former professor and vice president of the college. *Photo by Gayle Prince Rajtar.*

(16) ELIZABETH HALL

James Gamble Rogers II designed the three-story Elizabeth Hall dormitory, erected in 1958. It is more modern in style than most of the campus, but in 1967 the entrance was remodeled

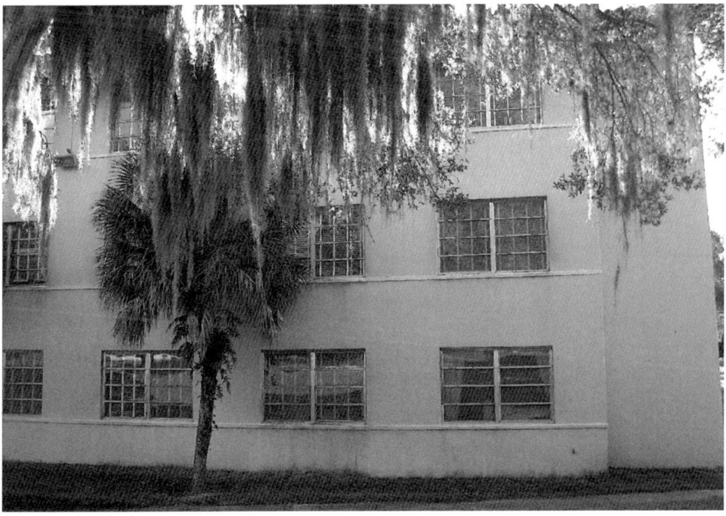

ELIZABETH HALL
Elizabeth Hall is a 145-bed coed dorm with separate floors and bathrooms for men and women. New students make up about one-third of its residents. The hall also houses the Dubois Health Center on its terrace level. *Photo by Gayle Prince Rajtar.*

with a more classic Spanish design. Jeannette McKean donated its furnishings and approved its naming to honor her mother, Elizabeth Morse Genius.

(17) FOX HALL

A loan from the PWA included funding for Fox Hall, built in 1936 as a women's dorm. It was the home of Phi Mu sorority and is now the home of Kappa Delta sorority. The hall is named for one of the college's benefactors, Caroline A. Fox.

Walk southeast on the sidewalk east of Elizabeth Hall.

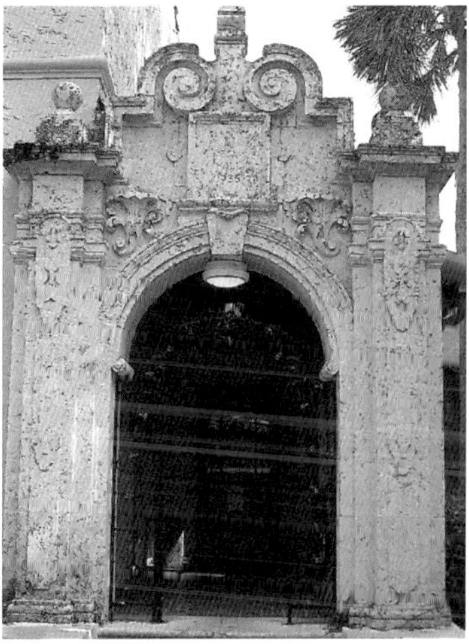

FOX HALL
The elaborate entranceway to Fox Hall was part of the Mediterranean-style building designed by Richard Kiehnel and John Elliott. It was redecorated in 2006 to bring the same style to its interior and was the first residence to do so. *Photo by Gayle Prince Rajtar.*

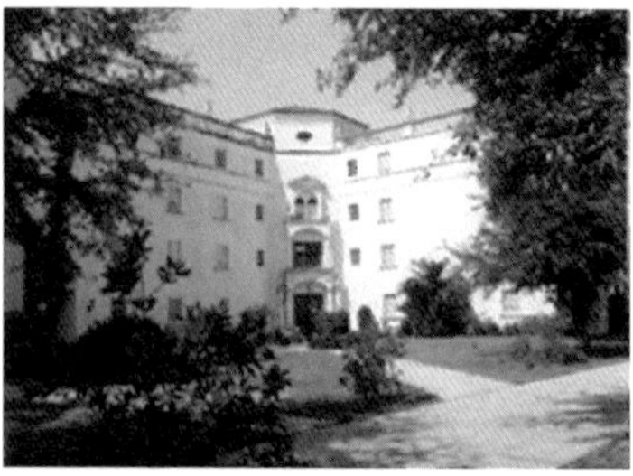

WARD HALL
Ward Hall was designed by Rogers, Lovelock and Fritz of Winter Park as a Mediterranean-style coed dormitory divided into wings, with only women on the second floor. About two-thirds of its residents are new students. *Courtesy of the Florida Photographic Collection.*

(18) WARD HALL

Called the New Women's Dorm upon its completion in 1970, this dorm was officially named George Morgan Ward Hall in honor of the third president of the college.

Head east on the sidewalk north of Ward Hall and then south on the sidewalk just to the east of it.

(19) FRENCH HOUSE

Funds for the French House were provided by Mabel Knowles Gage, the daughter of Francis Knowles, including a $50,000 endowment for its upkeep. The house is also known as La Maison Provençale and the Gage House.

Head north on the same sidewalk.

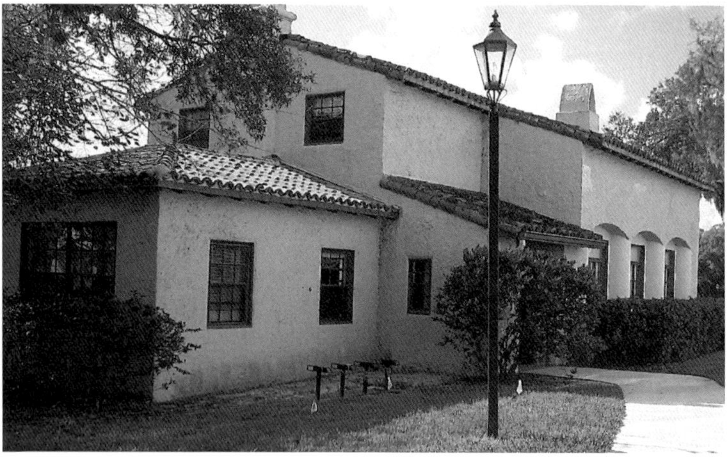

FRENCH HOUSE
The French House was dedicated in 1941 and was the first classroom designed specifically for the conference plan introduced by Hamilton Holt. Its purpose was to allow students to experience French culture on campus. *Photo by Gayle Prince Rajtar.*

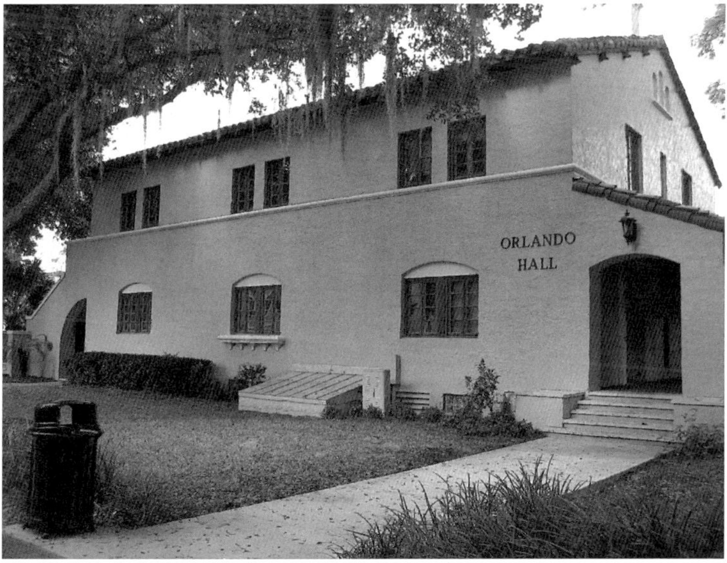

Orlando Hall
The dedication of Orlando Hall was held on April 6, 1949. The building contains faculty offices and several conference-style classrooms. *Photo by Gayle Prince Rajtar.*

(20) Orlando Hall

Orlando Hall was designed by George H. Spohn and was built in 1948 as part of the postwar Victory Expansion Program. A large portion of its cost was provided by residents of Orlando.

(21) Olin Library

In 1985, the Olin Library was built with funds granted by the F.W. Olin Foundation, which was created by ammunition manufacturer Franklin W. Olin in 1938. The foundation has provided buildings and equipment for fifty-seven independent college campuses.

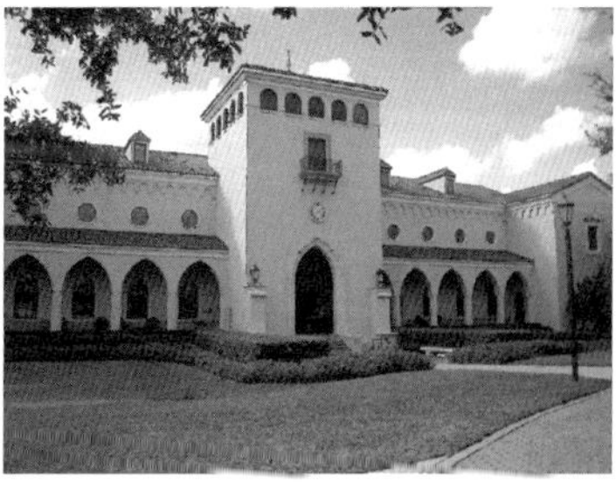

Olin Library
The Olin Library was built on the site of the second Knowles Hall and was designed by James Gamble Rogers II during the presidency of Thaddeus Seymour. A wing was added in 1998 for the Electronic Research and Information Center. *Photo by Gayle Prince Rajtar.*

(22) Cornell Campus Center

The Cornell Campus Center was built in 1999 and was designed by Shepley Bulfinch Richardson and Abbott of Boston. The initial $3 million donation for it came from 1935 Rollins graduate George D. Cornell and his wife Harriet.

(23) Alfond Swimming Pool

The campus pool was built in the early 1970s during the Critchfield administration. Construction of the Cornell Campus Center necessitated renovations to the pool in 1997. It is named for trustee Harold Alfond, who generously funded several sports facilities at Rollins.

Walk north on the sidewalk west of Cornell Campus Center.

(24) Woolson House

Clare A. Benedict donated $5,000 for the construction of the Constance Fenimore Woolson English House in memory of her aunt, an author. Benedict was also an author and was a grand-niece of novelist James Fenimore Cooper.

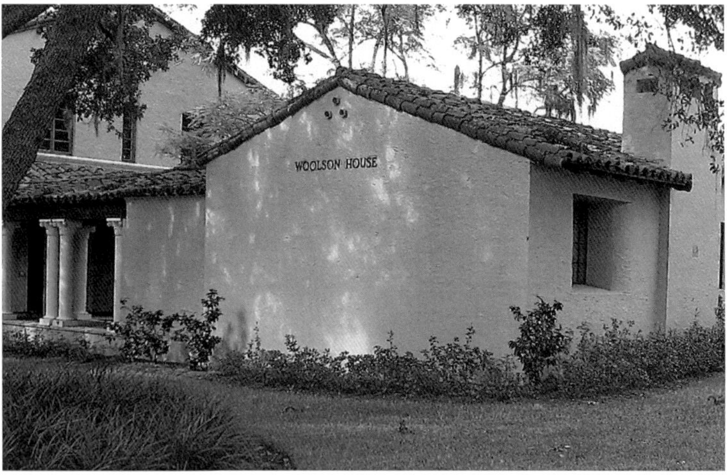

Woolson House

Benefactor Clare A. Benedict furnished the house with items from the estate of her aunt, author Constance Fenimore Woolson. In 1948, a loggia was built to connect it to Orlando Hall. Today, the house is used for literary workshops. *Photo by Gayle Prince Rajtar.*

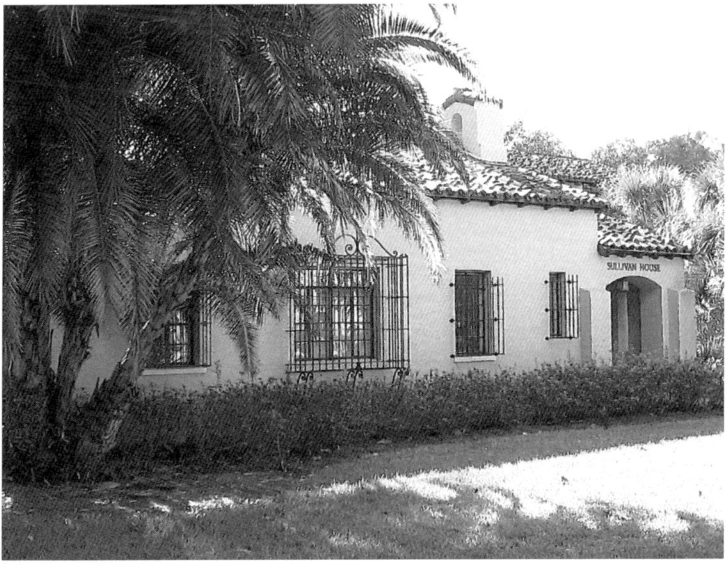

SULLIVAN HOUSE
The Sullivan House was dedicated in February 1948. Memorabilia, artwork and antiques from Algernon Sydney Sullivan and his son George are displayed there, along with a collection of items from Dr. and Mrs. Eugene R. Smith. *Photo by Gayle Prince Rajtar.*

(25) SULLIVAN HOUSE

Algernon Sydney Sullivan was a New York attorney who touched the lives of many. The Algernon Sydney Sullivan Awards were created in his memory for deserving students at Southern colleges and universities. A gift from the Algernon Sydney Sullivan Foundation, founded in 1934 by his son George, provided funding for the Sullivan House.

Head west on the sidewalk between the Woolson and Sullivan Houses.

(26) MARY JEAN MITCHELL PLAZA

The Mary Jean Mitchell Plaza was designed by local architect Scott Waldroff. It honors trustee Mary Jean Mitchell Green, who died in 1990 of breast cancer.

(27) TIEDTKE TENNIS COURTS

John Tiedtke helped rescue Rollins from the brink of financial disaster following the Holt administration in 1948 by leading a successful alumni fundraising campaign and securing a line of credit. He donated the Tiedtke Tennis Courts, was named a vice-president under Hugh McKean and also served as a faculty member and the president of the Bach Festival Society for forty-nine years.

Walk north on the sidewalk west of Mitchell Plaza.

(28) DYER MEMORIAL

The Dyer Memorial was built in 1939 by friends and admirers of Susan H. Dyer, the first director of the college's Conservatory of Music. The miniature concert hall designed by Richard Kiehnel is now used as a lounge.

Head west on Holt Avenue.

(29) CROSS HALL

In 1936, Cross Hall was completed and named to honor Lucy Cross, an Oberlin graduate and educator in Daytona. Her impassioned plea to create a college in Central Florida was presented to the Florida Congregationalist Association in 1884, planting the seed for Rollins College.

Walk east on Holt Avenue.

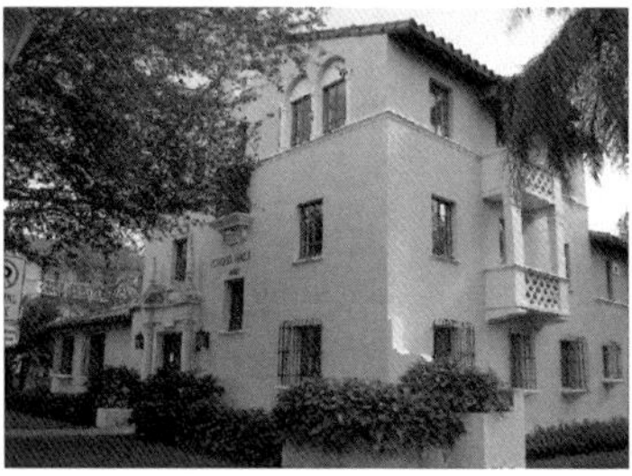

CROSS HALL
Cross Hall was designed by Richard Kiehnel and John Elliott in 1935 and was built with funds provided by the PWA as a women's dormitory. It shares a loggia and a lawn with Strong Hall and is the home of Alpha Omicron Pi, the newest sorority on campus. *Photo by Gayle Prince Rajtar.*

(30) MAYFLOWER HALL

Hamilton Holt suggested the name Mayflower Hall for the housing unit built with a $50,000 donation from Mr. and Mrs. Malcolm Forbes with the hope that he could acquire an artifact from the famed *Mayflower* pilgrim ship. He was eventually given a piece of timber by the British Society of Friends, along with a small fragment of Plymouth Rock given by Virginia Robie. Both are mounted on a plaque hanging over the fireplace mantel.

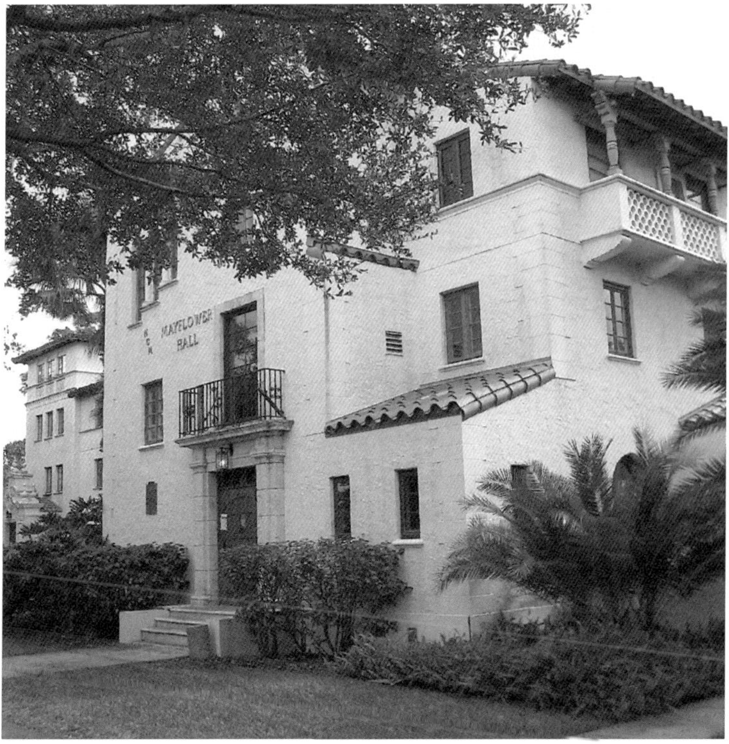

MAYFLOWER HALL
Richard Kiehnel designed this hall, which was built in 1930 as a women's dorm. It was occupied by Phi Beta Phi sorority from 1936 to 1970 and Phi Delta Theta fraternity from 1970 until the early 1990s, when Non Compis Mentis, the only Rollins local sorority, moved in. *Photo by Gayle Prince Rajtar.*

(31) PUGSLEY HALL

Trustee Cornelius A. Pugsley donated more than $43,000 to build Pugsley Hall in 1930. Its front wall bears a piece of stone taken from the foundation of the farmhouse in Peekskill, New York, where Pugsley was born.

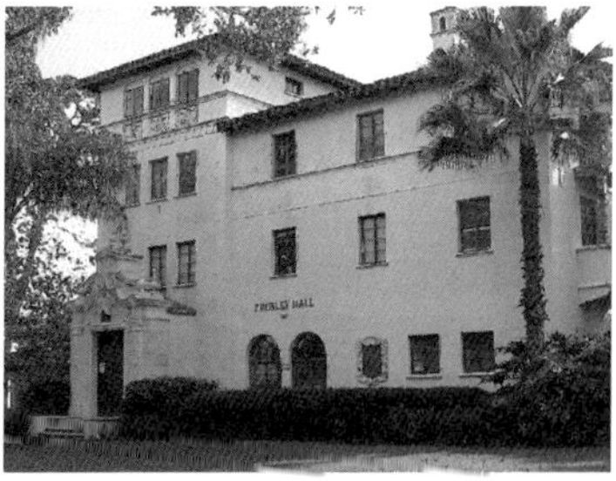

PUGSLEY HALL
Pugsley Hall, designed by Richard Kiehnel in the Mediterranean style, is one of the buildings along the "Rollins College Scenic Drive," which was later named Holt Avenue. Pugsley is the home of Tau Kappa Epsilon fraternity. *Photo by Gayle Prince Rajtar.*

(32) BEAL-MALTBIE CENTER

Altamonte Springs Mayor Birdsie L. Maltbie donated

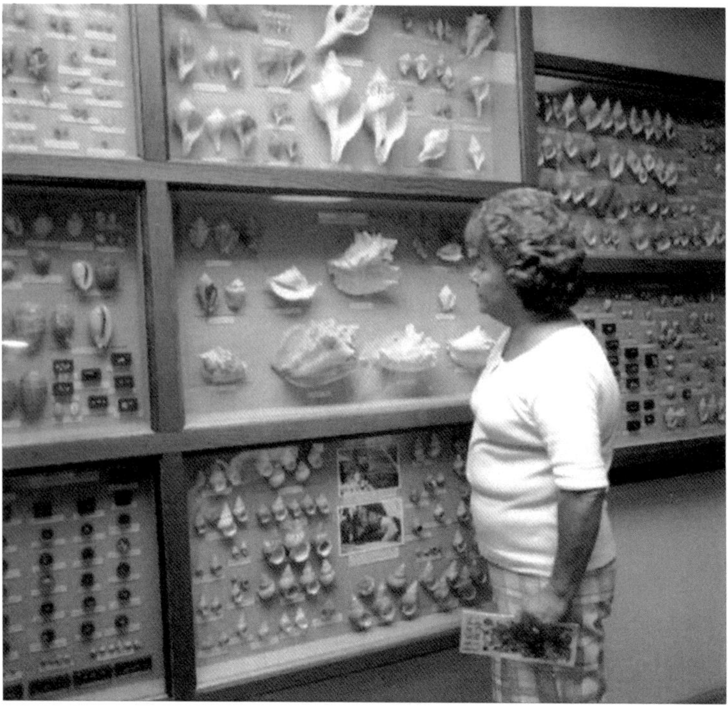

BEAL-MALTBIE CENTER
Harold Hair designed the Beal-Maltbie Shell Museum. It closed in the late 1980s when the shell collection was removed, and in 1991 it became the college's Center for Environmental Studies. *Courtesy of the Florida Photographic Collection.*

$10,000 for the construction of the Beal-Maltbie Shell Museum in 1941 to house the seashell collection of J.H. Beal of Merritt Island that was used for biological research.

(33) ALUMNI HOUSE

The Alumni House, designed by Richard Kiehnel of Coral Gables, was built in 1941. Hamilton Holt hired Kiehnel to create a master plan for the campus in the Spanish Mediterranean style popularized by Addison Mizner.

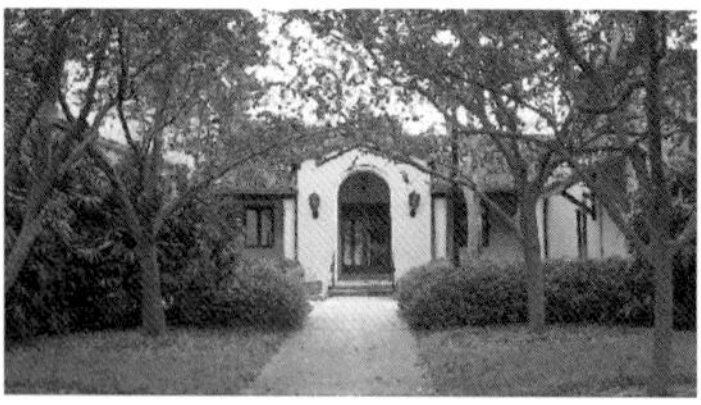

ALUMNI HOUSE
In 1967, Howard B. Fawcett Jr. of the Class of 1934 donated $2,000 to update the interior décor of the Alumni House, which features gifts from alumni. The house has office space for Rollins Alumni Inc. and is also a lounge for visiting alumni. *Photo by Gayle Prince Rajtar.*

(34) RICE FAMILY BOOKSTORE & CAFÉ

The Student Center was designed by Richard Kiehnel in 1941. Rollins alumni Charles E. Rice and his wife Dianne Tauscher Rice donated $1 million in 1998 for its complete renovation, restoring many original architectural elements. In 2000, the center reopened as the Rice Family Bookstore & Café.

(35) CARNEGIE HALL

Carnegie Hall was originally known as the Carnegie Library, built in 1911 with funds donated by Andrew Carnegie. Between 1881 and 1917, Carnegie helped establish libraries all over the world with over $56 million in endowments.

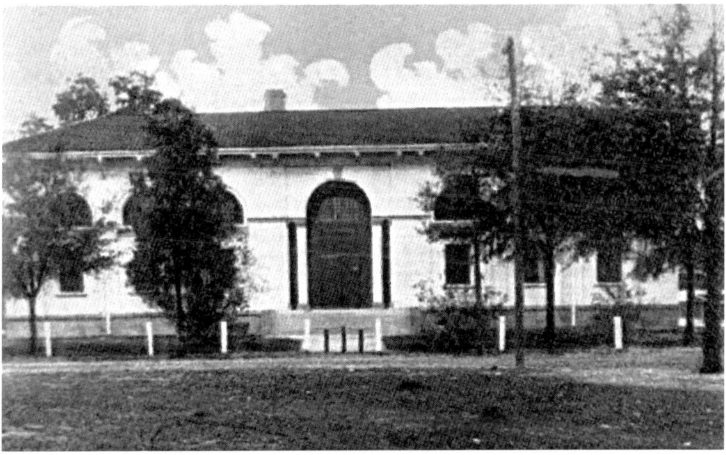

CARNEGIE HALL
Andrew Carnegie donated $20,000 for the construction of the library and granted $25,000 to rebuild Knowles Hall, on the condition that his funds were matched by other sources. Knowles II was used until 1984, when it was replaced by the Olin Library. *Courtesy of the Florida Photographic Collection.*

(36) NELSON ROSE GARDEN

Virginia S. Nelson and her husband W.W. Nelson moved to Winter Park in 1940 and became generous donors to the college. A rose garden located adjacent to the Warren Administration Building was dedicated in Virginia's memory in 1994.

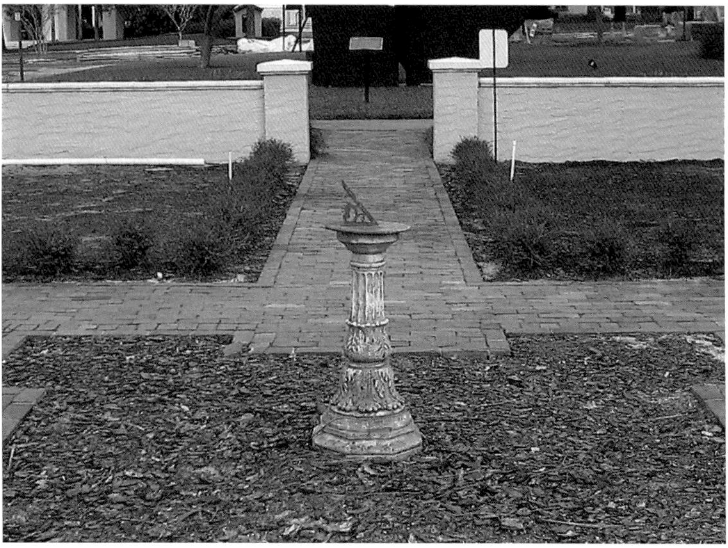

NELSON ROSE GARDEN
The Virginia S. Nelson Rose Garden features a sundial in the center of the square, walled garden with brick walkways throughout. The dedication plaque mentions "her love of children, music, art, dogs, camellias and roses." *Photo by Gayle Prince Rajtar.*

(37) WARREN ADMINISTRATION BUILDING

George H. Spohn designed the Warren Administration Building in 1946 and its builder was Harry C. Cone. It was dedicated in 1947 and was a gift from Mrs. George E. Warren.

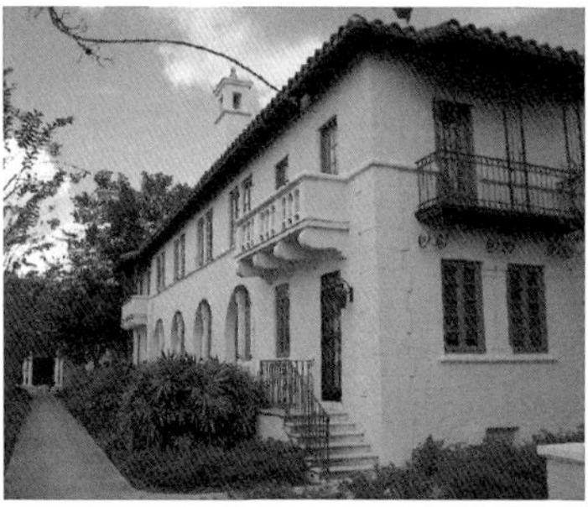

WARREN ADMINISTRATION BUILDING
During the McKean presidency the Warren Administration Building was called the "Pink Palace" because of its bright pink color. *Photo by Gayle Prince Rajtar.*.

(38) WALK OF FAME

Hamilton Holt's Walk of Fame was inspired by "ancestral walks" taken with his father in New England. The walk, dedicated on October 18, 1929, was composed of twenty-two stones symbolizing persons of national or international prominence and came from their birthplaces, former homes, gravesites or places closely associated with them.

Head south and east along the Horseshoe.

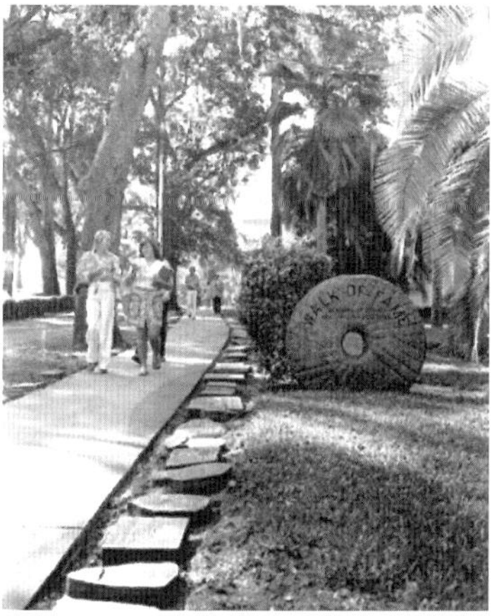

WALK OF FAME

The millstone at the head of the Walk of Fame came from Gauge Hall, part of Hamilton Holt's home in Connecticut. Notables represented include George Washington, Henry Wadsworth Longfellow, Dolley Madison, Edgar Allan Poe, Mark Twain and Rollins graduate Fred Rogers. *Courtesy of the Florida Photographic Collection.*

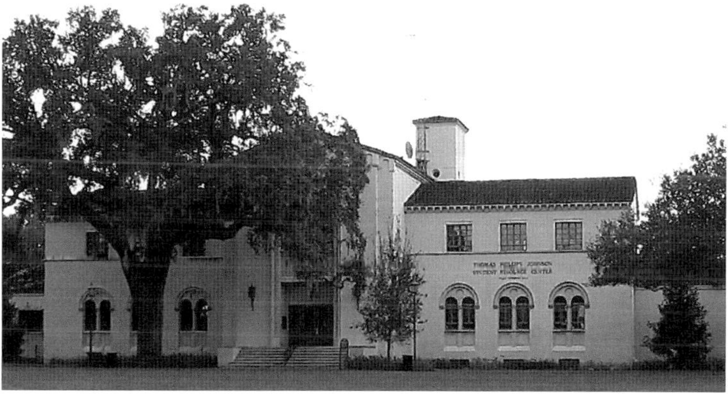

MILLS MEMORIAL CENTER

The Mills Memorial Center houses the student government offices and WPRK, the college radio station. It is also the office of the student newspaper, *The Sandspur*, which debuted in 1894 and continues today as the oldest college newspaper in Florida. *Photo by Gayle Prince Rajtar.*

(39) MILLS MEMORIAL CENTER

A $500,000 donation from the Davella Mills Foundation provided funding for the Mills Memorial Library, now known as the Mills Memorial Center. Construction began in the summer of 1950 and was completed in 1951.

Continue east along the Horseshoe.

(40) CHASE HALL

Chase Hall was designed by Whitfield and King of New York in 1908 and was built by W.R. Richardson and Company of

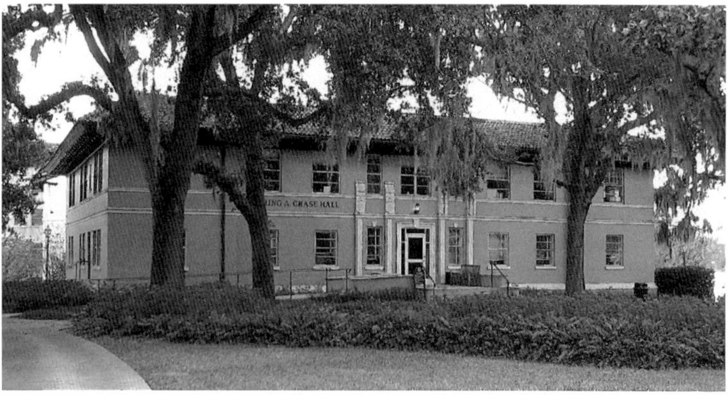

Chase Hall

Chase Hall housed military intelligence trainees during World War II and was later used as a women's dorm to accommodate a record number of female students. Two fraternities occupied Chase Hall—Sigma Phi Epsilon from 1966 to 1999 and Phi Delta Theta from 2002 to 2003. The building is used today for offices, including a student leadership organization. *Photo by Gayle Prince Rajtar.*

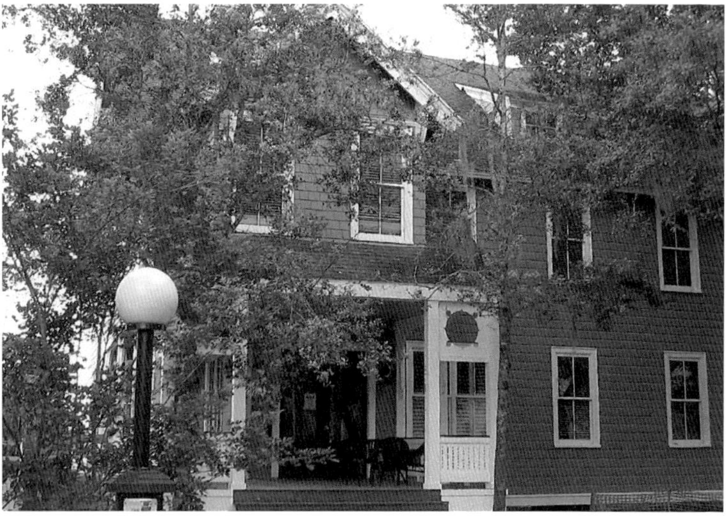

Pinehurst Hall

In 2007, Pinehurst Cottage was renovated in an effort to restore its original décor inside and out. Wheelchair access was also added. Residents of this hall are chosen for their dedication to special interests outside the classroom. *Photo by Gayle Prince Rajtar.*

Jacksonville. A $10,000 gift from the estate of Loring Chase and gifts from supporters funded the men's dorm that was built as a memorial to one of the founders of Winter Park.

Head northeast along the Horseshoe.

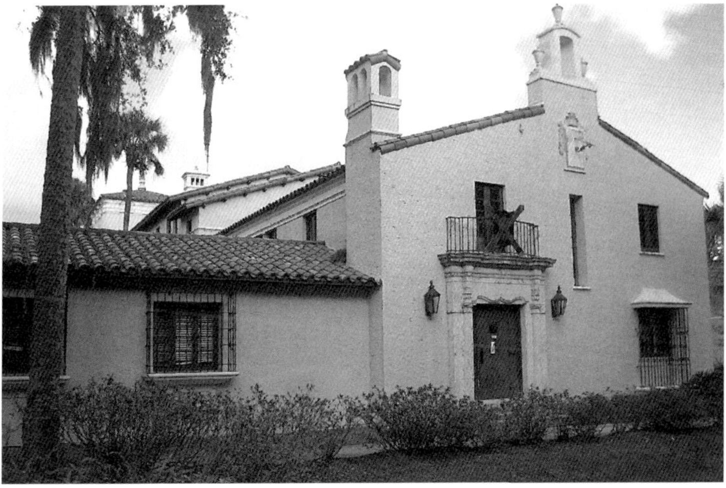

Gale Hall

Gale Hall has housed several fraternities, including the current residents, the members of X-Club, which was created by Hamilton Holt for non-fraternity students and transfer students from non-represented fraternities. *Photo by Gayle Prince Rajtar.*

(41) Pinehurst Hall

Pinehurst Cottage for women was built in 1886 with funds provided by Francis Knowles and was designed by George D. Rand.

Head north along the Horseshoe.

(42) Gale Hall

In 1936, Richard Kiehnel designed Gale Hall, another building funded by the PWA. It was named in honor of Sullivan F. Gale, one of the original trustees.

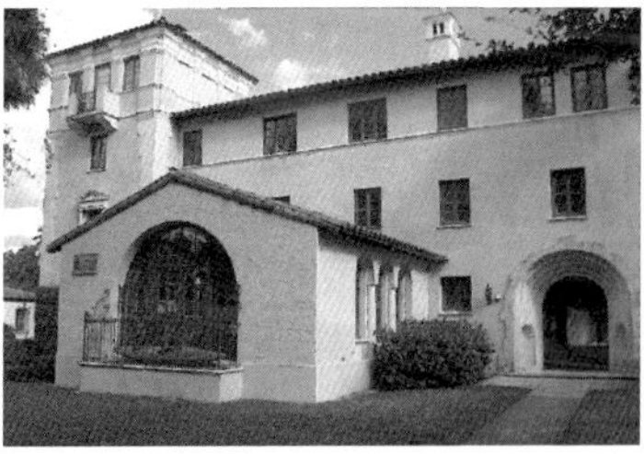

Lyman Hall

Several fraternities have called Lyman Hall home, including X Club, Phi Delta Theta and Delta Chi. The Outdoor Club currently resides there and is a group dedicated to outdoor activities. *Photo by Gayle Prince Rajtar.*

(43) Lyman Hall

Funding for Lyman Hall was provided by the PWA. It was designed by Richard Kiehnel, was built in 1936 and was dedicated in honor of Frederick Lyman in 1937.

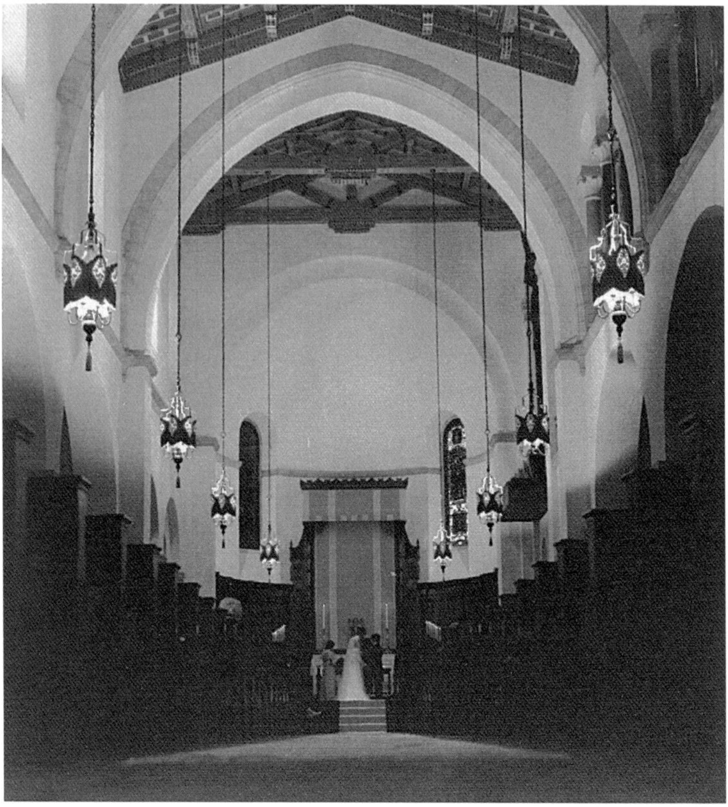

Knowles Memorial Chapel

Knowles Memorial Chapel, also known as the Rollins Chapel, has long been a popular place for Rollins students and alumni to get married. Shown here in a photo from June 15, 1974, is the wedding ceremony of the authors of this book. *From the authors' collection.*

(44) Knowles Memorial Chapel

Knowles Memorial Chapel was designed by Ralph Adams Cram, who also designed the nation's largest cathedral, St. John the Divine in New York City, and the University of Notre Dame chapel. Construction was completed in 1932 with funds donated by Frances Knowles Warren in memory of her father, Francis Knowles.

Continue east on Holt Avenue.

(45) Hooker Hall

Richard Kiehnel designed Hooker Hall, which was built in 1936 by Harry C. Cone with funds provided by the PWA. The hall was named for the first president of Rollins, who presided over the first commencement exercises in May 1890.

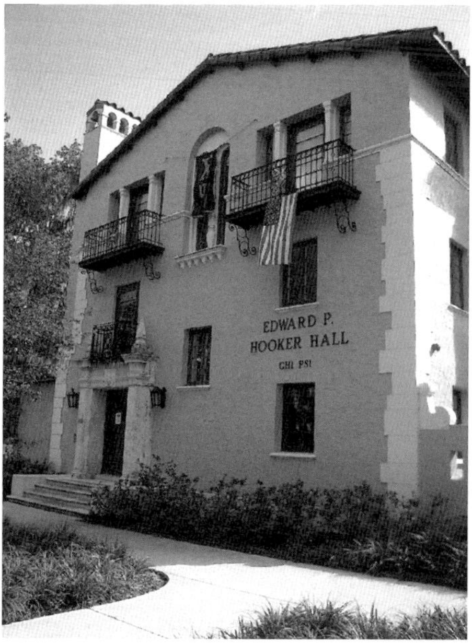

Right:

HOOKER HALL

Residents of Hooker Hall have included the following fraternities: Theta Kappa Nu, Lambda Chi Alpha, Lambda, Lambda Chi Psi and the current residents, Chi Psi. *Photo by Gayle Prince Rajtar.*

Below:

ROLLINS HALL

Rollins Hall originally was a men's housing unit for Rho Lambda Nu, Sigma Nu and Delta Chi. It is now used by Kappa Kappa Gamma sorority. *Photo by Gayle Prince Rajtar.*

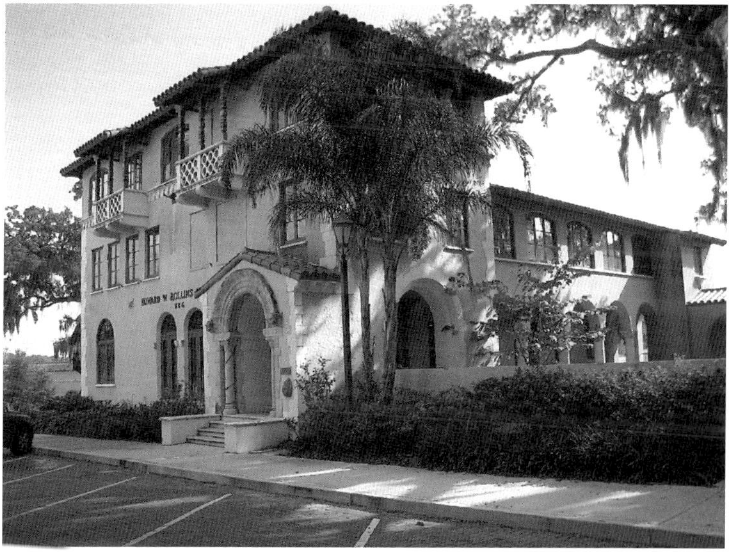

(46) ROLLINS HALL

Rollins Hall was designed by Richard Kichnel in 1929, the first of Hamilton Holt's Spanish-Mediterranean style for the campus, and was dedicated in 1930. The primary donor was Boston banker Edward W. Rollins, a cousin of Alonzo Rollins.

Walk south on the road east of Rollins Hall.

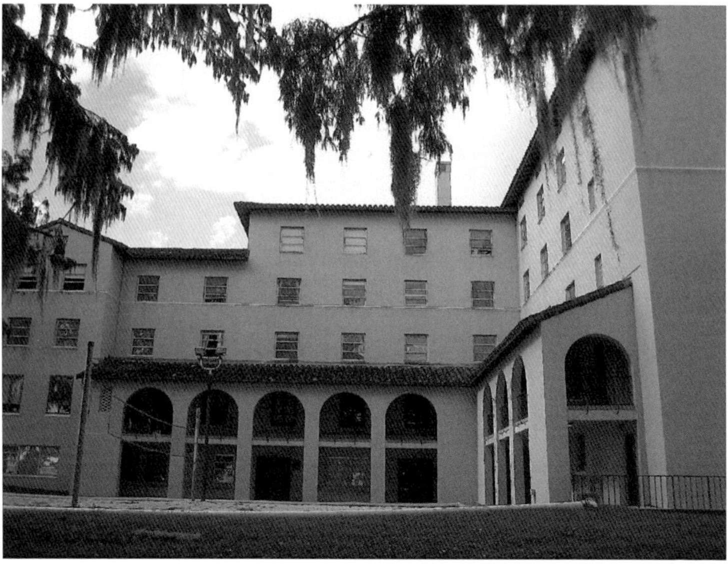

MCKEAN HALL
The H.J. High Construction Company of Orlando built McKean Hall, which was designed by Rogers, Lovelock and Fritz. It has been a men's dorm and has been used by Kappa Delta sorority, but it is now a coed dorm for new honors students and those participating in the Nexus Learning Community. *Photo by Gayle Prince Rajtar.*

(47) MCKEAN HALL

McKean Hall was built using a government loan of over $1 million in 1962 and was originally called New Hall. The name was changed in 1974 to honor the tenth president, Hugh McKean.

Continue north on the same road.

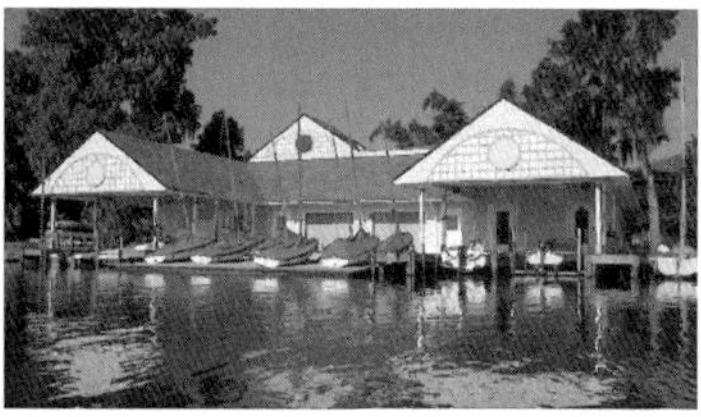

ALFOND BOATHOUSE
The Alfond Boathouse is named for Harold Alfond, a generous supporter of the college with two sons who graduated from Rollins. This half-million-dollar facility contains a classroom, locker room and other amenities for watersports. *Photo by Steve Rajtar.*

(48) ALFOND BOATHOUSE

The Lake Virginia Boathouse was built in 1904 and was used until it was damaged by Hurricane Donna in 1960. It was rebuilt the following year by Hugh McKean and was in use until it was demolished and replaced by the Alfond Boathouse in 1990.

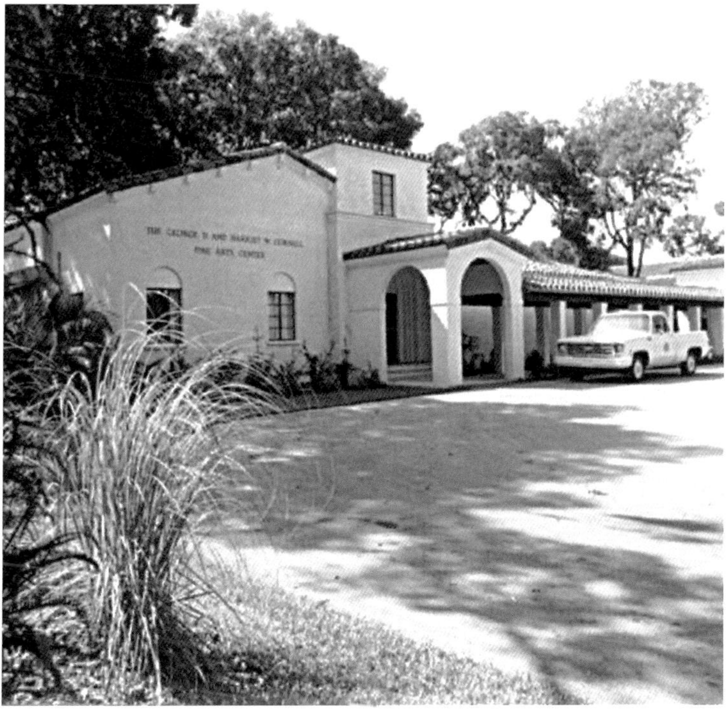

CORNELL FINE ARTS MUSEUM
The Cornell Fine Arts Museum reopened in January 2006 after a year and a half of renovations that nearly doubled its size. Today the museum is considered to be one of the finest college art museums in the country, with one of the oldest and most prestigious collections in Florida. *Courtesy of the Florida Photographic Collection.*

(49) CORNELL ART CENTER

The Cornell Art Center is part of the fine arts complex and was built with more than $1 million from George and Harriet Cornell in 1976. It opened in 1978 and is currently home to the Rollins Art and Art History Department.

(50) CORNELL FINE ARTS MUSEUM

Ground was broken for what would become the Cornell Fine Arts Museum in 1975. The Jessie Ball DuPont Fund and generous donations from George and Harriet Cornell provided funding, and the museum opened in 1978.

Head west on the north side of Holt Avenue.

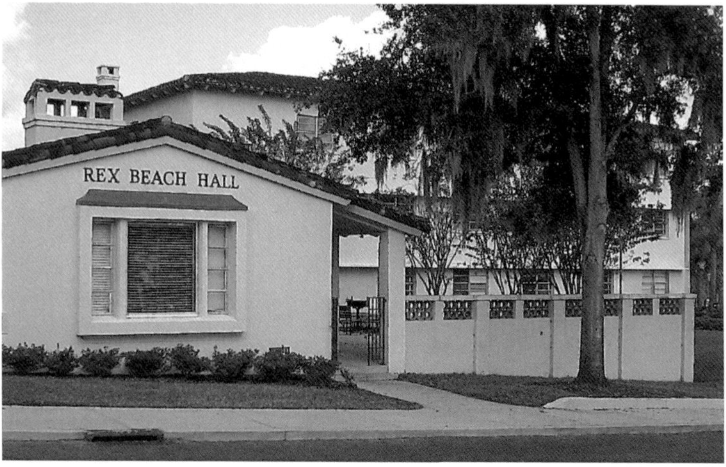

Rex Beach Hall
Kappa Alpha and Phi Delta Theta have resided in Rex Beach Hall. The hall is now a coed Living Learning Community enabling students in the arts to live, study and socialize in a common environment. *Photo by Gayle Prince Rajtar.*

(51) Rex Beach Hall

In 1957, Rex Beach Hall was designed by John T. Watson and was named for writer Rex Beach, who attended the prep school in the early days of Rollins College. Beach never graduated from the college, but he was presented with two honorary degrees by Hamilton Holt and was president of the Rollins Alumni Association from 1927 until 1940. A marble slab marks the site where the ashes of Beach and his wife were interred.

(52) Keene Hall

Schweizer Associates were the architects for Keene Hall, which was built in 1974, and the contractor was Allen Trovillion. Funds were donated by Mr. and Mrs. Fred Rogers and the McFeely-Rogers Foundation, the Kresge Foundation and the Keene Family Foundation, which provided the largest share. The building was named in honor of R.D. Keene, a leader in the Florida citrus industry.

Continue west on Holt Avenue and head north on Chase Avenue.

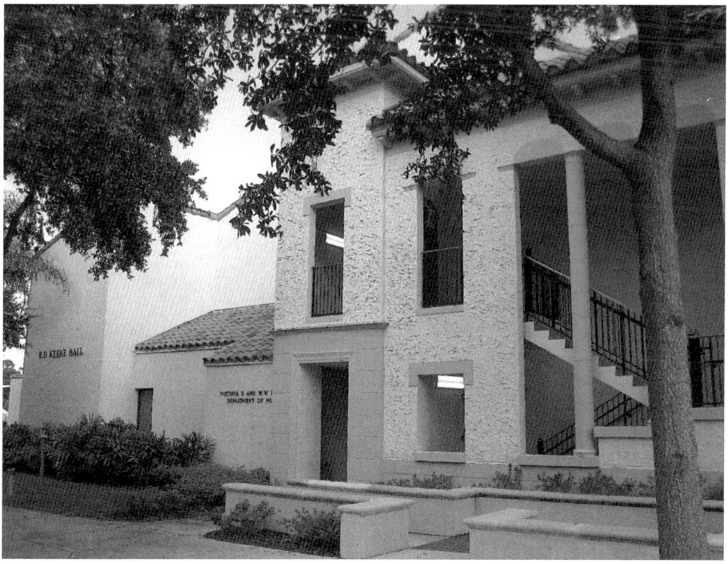

KEENE HALL

Keene Hall holds the Virginia S. and W.W. Nelson Department of Music and features the state of the art John Tiedtke Concert Hall, which was added during renovations in 2005. *Photo by Gayle Prince Rajtar.*

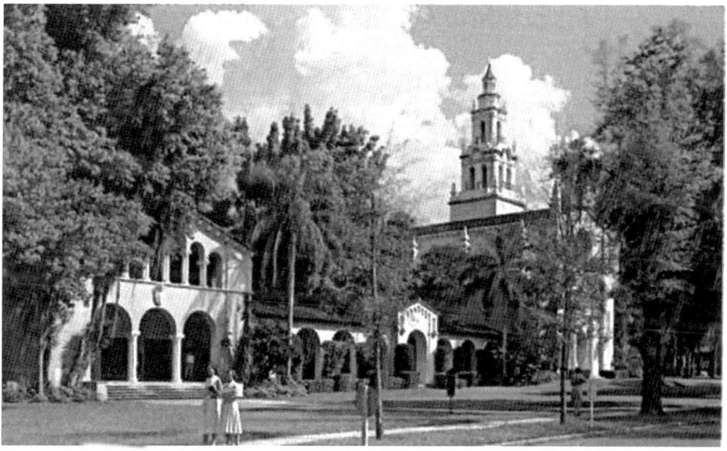

ANNIE RUSSELL THEATRE

In 1931, Richard Kiehnel designed the Annie Russell Theatre to connect to Knowles Memorial Chapel and both were built at the same time. The theatre was dedicated in the spring of 1932 and was added to the National Register in 1998. *Courtesy of the Florida Photographic Collection.*

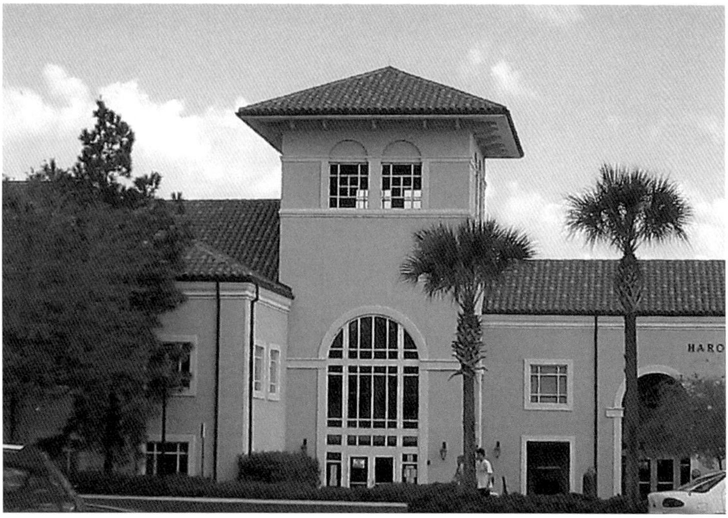

ALFOND SPORTS CENTER
Construction of the Alfond Sports Center began in 1999 and the facility opened in December of 2000. The center provides more than twice the space of the former field house and includes the Warden Performance Arena, the McKean Gymnasium, Daryl's Fitness Center, classrooms, offices and a Hall of Fame section. *Photo by Gayle Prince Rajtar.*

(53) ANNIE RUSSELL THEATRE

Internationally renowned British actress Annie Russell retired from the New York stage to Winter Park in 1918. She became involved in the budding theatre program at Rollins College at the urging of her wealthy friend and admirer Mary Curtis Bok Zimbalist, whose donation of $100,000 funded the Annie Russell Theatre with the proviso that Russell would serve as the director so long as she was able.

(54) ALFOND SPORTS CENTER

The former Enyart-Alumni Field House, built in 1967, was the foundation for the Harold and Ted Alfond Sports Center. The father and son created a $3 million challenge grant to establish the building fund in 1996 with additional funds provided by alumni and friends of the college, including the Elizabeth Morse Genius Foundation and the Bert W. Martin Foundation.

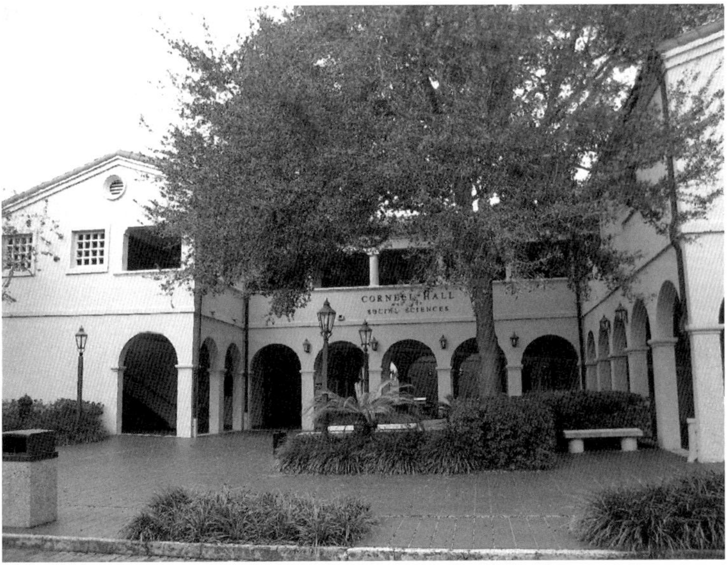

CORNELL HALL FOR SOCIAL SCIENCES
Cornell Hall houses the Social Science Department and includes classrooms and offices. Rita Bornstein's Campaign for Rollins included the largest single donation in the school's history, $93.3 million from the estate of Rollins alumnus George Cornell. *Photo by Gayle Prince Rajtar.*

(55) CORNELL HALL

Harriet and George Cornell provided the funding for Cornell Hall, which was built in 1987 and was designed by Rogers, Lovelock and Fritz. The dedication ceremony in 1988 included the placement of a time capsule behind the cornerstone intended to be opened a hundred years later.

(56) FRED STONE THEATRE

Fred Stone was a beloved and talented actor whose career began in a circus and grew to include medicine shows, minstrel acts, musical comedy, theatre and film. His appearance in a special performance of *Lightnin'* in 1939 raised enough money for the college to purchase an old sorority house, which became the original Fred Stone Theatre. The current location was originally the First Baptist Church of Winter Park and was built in 1926.

Continue north on Chase Avenue and head east on Fairbanks Avenue and south on Ollie Avenue to the beginning of the tour.

Part IV

Additional Historic Sites

565 West Fairbanks Avenue

Harper's Tavern Building

This two-story building opened in 1927 as a feed store. In 1932, it became Harper's Tavern, a popular nightspot for college students and local residents. On June 4, 1996, the building (which also housed the Cordon Bleu Restaurant) was severely damaged by fire. Restoration included a new brick front, and now it is the home of O'Boy's Bar-B-Q.

746 Formosa Avenue

Kress Memorial Seventh-Day Adventist Church

This church is named for Lauretta E. and Daniel H. Kress, who studied medicine at the Seventh-Day Adventist College in Battle Creek. After graduating in 1894, they founded sanitariums in England, Australia and the United States. One in Maryland was the Washington Sanitarium and Hospital where, in 1907, Lauretta became Montgomery County's first female physician and surgeon. There, in 1916, she opened a maternity ward and personally delivered more than five thousand babies. Daniel served as its first medical director. They later retired to Orlando.

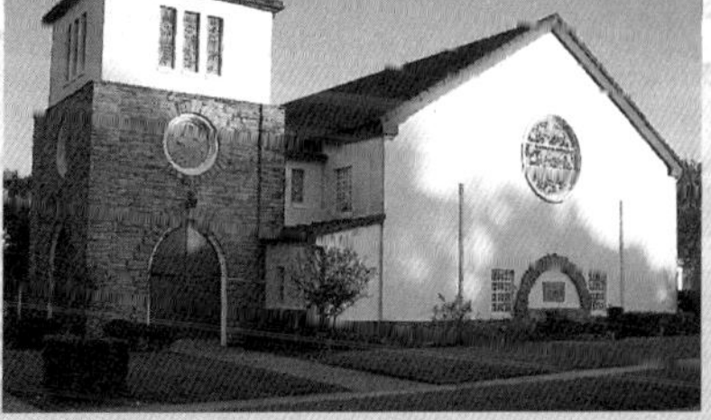

KRESS MEMORIAL CHURCH
This church was named to honor a pair of doctors who practiced in several states and countries. They worked to spread information about the dangers of tobacco products as early as 1915, and coauthored the 1932 book, *Under the Guiding Hand.* *Photo by Steve Rajtar.*

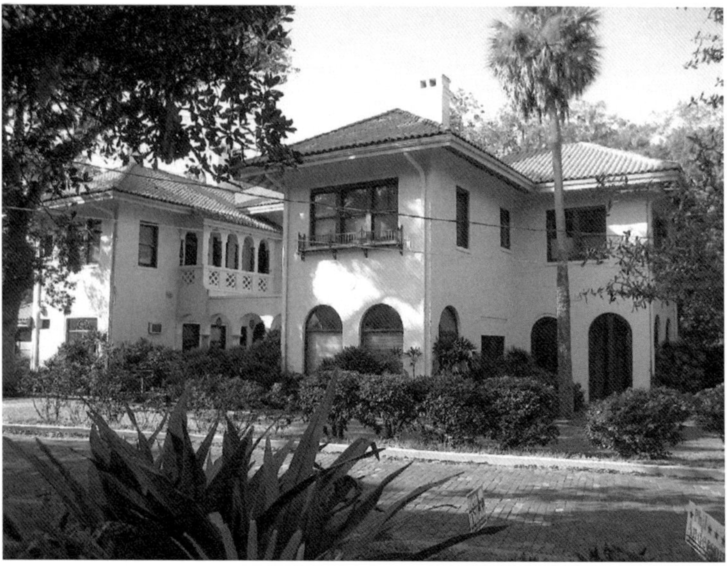

RANDALL HOUSE
This is Ripples II, the imposing home at the west end of Spring Lane that was used as a location for the filming of the 1975 movie, *The Meal*, starring Dina Merrill and Carl Betz. After its run in theaters, it was released on video under the name *Deadly Encounter*. *Photo by Steve Rajtar.*

2400 FORREST ROAD

RANDALL HOUSE

The home called Ripples I was built in 1910 by Judge Isaac Hopper. In 1923, Walter Randall replaced the original home with the present Mediterranean-style mansion, which cost $180,000. It has poured reinforced concrete walls that are eighteen inches thick. Ceilings are thirteen feet tall and there are six fireplaces. The Randalls lived in the home until 1952.

Bibliography

Baker, Mrs. Robert S. *Tombstone Inscriptions, Palm Cemetery, Winter Park, Florida.* Winter Park, FL: W.P. Duval Chapter DAR, 1960.

Blackman, William Fremont. *History of Orange County, Florida: Narrative and Biographical.* DeLand, FL: E.O. Painter Printing Co., 1927.

Campen, Richard N. *Winter Park Portrait: The Story of Winter Park and Rollins College.* Beachwood, OH: West Summit Press, 1987.

Chapman, Robin. *The Absolutely Essential Guide to Winter Park.* Winter Park, FL. Absolutely Essential Company, 2001.

———. *Winter Park in Vintage Postcards.* Charleston, SC: Arcadia Publishing, 2005.

Conn, Stetson. *The Episcopal Church in Winter Park, Florida, 1883–1983.* Orlando, FL: Moran Printing Company, 1984.

Douglass, Harry S. *First Congregational Church of Winter Park, Florida, 1884–1984.* Winter Park: Florida Press, 1984.

Gray, W. Breathitt, Jr. *A History of the First United Methodist Church of Winter Park, Florida.* Orlando, FL: Ferris Printing Co., 1972.

Hall, Clyde W. *An African-American Growing Up On the West Side of Winter Park, Florida 1925–1942.* Winter Park, FL: Clyde W. Hall, 2005.

Jammal, S.E., and Barry F. Beck. *A Self-Guided Field Trip to the Winter Park Sinkhole.* Orlando: Florida Sinkhole Research Institute, 1985.

MacDowell, Claire Leavitt. *Chronological History of Winter Park.* Winter Park, FL: Orange Press, 1950.

McClane, Patrick W. and Debra A. *The Architecture of James Gamble Rogers II in Winter Park, Florida.* Gainesville: University Press of Florida, 2004.

Schenck, Noella LaChance. *Winter Park's Old Alabama Hotel.* Winter Park, FL: Anna Publishing, Inc., 1982.

Stark, William E. *The First Twenty-Five Years of the University Club of Winter Park.* Winter Park, FL: William E. Stark, 1959.

Strong, Hope, Jr. *Tales of Winter Park.* Orlando, FL: Rollins Press, 1982.

Sully, Susan. *Casa Florida: Spanish-Style Houses from Winter Park to Coral Gables.* New York: Rizzoli International Publications, Inc., 2005.

Zhang, Wenxian, David Smith, and Patricia Strout. *Walk of Fame: A Rollins Legacy.* Winter Park, FL: Rollins College, 2003.

Index

About the Authors

Steve Rajtar grew up near Cleveland, Ohio, came to Florida for college, earned degrees in mathematics, anthropology, law and taxation and decided to stay. He has had fifteen books published prior to this one, all dealing in some fashion with history, including historical guides for several Central Florida cities. He also leads tours of Winter Park and other cities on foot, bicycle and kayak.

Gayle Prince Rajtar was born in Orlando into a family that moved to the city a hundred years ago. She earned a degree in communications while working as a professional singer and drummer, and has remained an Orlando resident. As a freshman at Rollins College in 1971, she met Steve in front of Knowles Memorial Chapel, and they were married there in 1974.

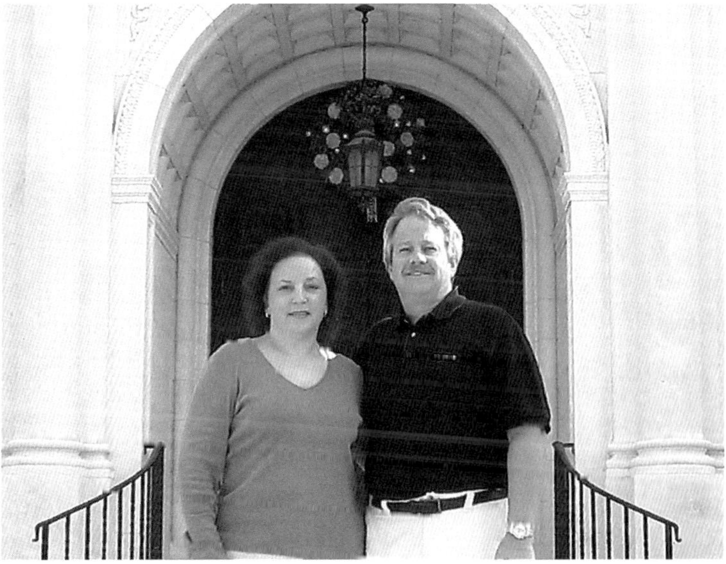

The authors on the steps of Knowles Memorial Chapel. *Photo by the authors.*

Visit us at
www.historypress.net.